MW01532416

NARCISSISM IN THE WORKPLACE

WHAT IT IS
HOW TO SPOT IT
WHAT TO DO ABOUT IT

by

Dr. Samuel Grier, Ph.D.

TABLE OF CONTENTS

INTRODUCTION

You may be reading this book to learn what narcissism is all about. You may be reading it because you already know what narcissism is, and you want to learn more about the personality traits associated with someone who has a narcissistic personality disorder.

Maybe you are reading it because you have intellectual curiosity.

Or perhaps you think you work with a narcissist and you don't know what to do, you don't know how to cope. If that is why you picked up this book, then you and I and others who have worked with a narcissist have a special connection. We understand each other and can identify with what each of us has been through — and yet we are disappointed when we cannot convey to our friends and family and professional associates what it means to work with someone who is a narcissist in the truest sense of the word.

I hope that the account in this book changes that. I hope that this brief chronicle tells "our" story.

I am not a psychologist, and I never intended to write a book like this. I would rather write fiction. But working with a narcissist forever changes his unfortunate coworkers, and the experience certainly changed me.

All right. Enough small talk. Let's commiserate.

PROLOGUE

I was happily working at a high performing and fast moving organization in a large international company when the events described in this story took place. While I avoid identifying the organization that I worked for and I have changed the names of my coworkers, I want to create an equivalent context for events as they unfold. So let me tell you a little about the environment in which I worked and my organization's purpose in life.

Twice a year our company sponsored a six-month course for eighty up-and-coming corporate managers. The group physically moved to our location and for that period formed professional relationships and personal bonds that would benefit both the company and the careers of the participants. My organization's charter was to expose the participants on the course to the major issues affecting our business, thus preparing them for future leadership. I was Director, responsible for the academic side of the program: its content, its execution and supporting educational methodologies. I also had a research division under my purview that explored corporate-wide trends and conducted analyses. I had a counterpart on the support side who took care of human resources and the infrastructure side of our activities (both facilities and technical). Al, our boss, had overall responsibility for the course and answered to the Board of Directors for how it served the interests of the company. We also sponsored at our location a number of short courses, conferences and ad hoc events on behalf of other offices.

Under me were two key executive positions. One had oversight of the material used in the course to include its relevance and its production, and was responsible for the recruitment of experts or senior practitioners to lecture to the participants. The other had responsibility for the day to day execution of the course. Each executive was supported by members of a "combined staff" and given appropriate administrative assistance.

I loved my job. I had led many successful groups, and this time was no exception. I had competed hard to get my position, and the work was everything that I thought it would be. I knew many of the people on the support side having worked with them before, and my arrival had literally been like coming home.

In close cooperation with my boss, Al, we had already significantly transformed the office and had much more in mind. The days were exciting, the activities fulfilling, and it seemed that the future guaranteed more of the same. Dick, my counterpart on the human resources and support side, had arrived shortly after me, and he brought unusual energy and innovation to his job. He joined with Al and me to create unprecedented cooperation and develop a joint vision for the office.

And then it happened.

Ken arrived and filled one of the key executive positions under me. He was well known in the business, and he was considered highly qualified. Physically, he was tall with classic good looks. Intellectually, he was brilliant. He spoke several languages, all of them fluently. On paper he was a perfect fit for our office — anyone's office, really.

But Ken was a narcissist. I would discover the implications of that realization one painful step at a time, and that is what makes this story different.

I won't be telling you what makes someone a narcissist. Rather, you will walk with me through my experience with Ken from hopeful beginning to bitter end — the confusion, the emotions, the attempts to cope, the relief when we finally parted ways. And when it is over, we will recap together what we learned by establishing ten rules for how to cope with someone afflicted with a narcissistic personality disorder.

CHAPTER 1

The Arrival

The kind of high level person I'm going to be talking about has typically been successful in his field. He is usually well liked by peers outside the office. He is cultured. Witty. Memorizes lots of little ditties and quotes that prominent people have said previously to distinguished audiences.

I learned to be amazed at what a person with a true narcissistic personality disorder could improvise on the spot. The amusing sayings. The trivia. The stories of his association with well-known or prominent personalities, and how he was sure that he had said something that had a profound effect on them. How he "shined" as the center of attention. How he was able to dominate every conversation and discussion of which he was a part.

I had never encountered this kind of individual before and was wholly unprepared for the experience that would forever change my view of the workplace. The same would be true with my boss. It would be a most unfortunate lesson in leadership for both of us that would spoil the last two years that we worked together. Not to mention the impact it had on everyone else in the office.

What do they say? Misery loves company? This I would not wish on anyone.

The Rumors

The new guy, Ken, who had been hired to work for me in one of my two key positions was identified by the higher-ups, and his résumé was impressive. "He'll be an asset for sure," I remember thinking. A colleague from another office whose opinion I valued had called and mentioned that he had worked with Ken's office in the past and that he enjoyed Ken's company socially.

But in contrast to these glowing reports, the secretary buzz had taken on a sour flavor.

"I have a friend who works with the new hire," my personal assistant said as I returned to the office from a meeting.

"Really?" I asked only half listening, stopping and raising my eyebrows to indicate that I heard what she said and to give her a chance to fill me in on the gossip.

"No one is willing to work with him. He can't get a job anywhere else. He's been told that either he comes here or he'll have to retire."

Gossip. Rumors. Why would our office be singled out to be the victim of a "body shuffle"?

"I wonder why that is," I remarked, giving my assistant an opportunity to provide more detail.

"They can't wait for him to leave," she said, knowing that she had my attention. "My friend says you can't disagree with him. It's his way or the highway."

"He seems to be well qualified," I gently protested. Mentally I went through his résumé once more.

"They pushed him out," she said. "And he didn't want to come here."

"He's coming for an interview. It's only a formality, but I'll keep my antennae up."

But my wariness was short lived.

Narcissists have this way of putting you at ease when you first meet. They are so well spoken. So intelligent. They have a veneer of charm and charisma.

It is only when the veneer is peeled away that you see the narcissist for what he is. But by the time that you realize there is a problem, it is too late. He has already been at work, unbeknownst to you.

And much to your chagrin, he is just getting started.

The Interview

I suppose in retrospect that a psychologist would have been aghast.

Had my wife done the interview, I know she would have asked why the new hire was being allowed to come to our location. She happens to have a degree in counseling, but even before her education and training she could size people up in a matter of a single, brief conversation.

In a previous position, if it was possible I always had her meet people before I made the decision to hire them. Although we had a thorough hiring process at the office and my number two had been a "people person", I found it useful to have her opinion. Long conversations were better, but I was amazed at what she could tell me after even a brief superficial introduction during a social activity.

"Did you get that?" she'd ask.

"Get what?" I'd say.

And then I'd get an earful. Sometimes good, sometimes bad. Health-related characteristics I might have never noticed and personality traits I would not have detected on my own. Her intuition and power of observation would give me something to follow up the next day, and my wife was almost always right. She had been right about Ken, too, but unfortunately for me she did not meet him until several months after he arrived.

At the first social occasion where colleagues from other offices had a chance to meet him, a longtime acquaintance looked at me after being subjected to a five-minute monologue from Ken and asked, "Who the *expletive* was that?"

Another colleague would remark to me that "No matter where a conversation with Ken starts, I am amazed that he always manages to end up talking about himself."

Feedback on his participation in various forums that were part of our six-month course was always negative. "We have only fifty minutes to discuss the issue of the day, and when Ken sits in on our sessions he talks for forty minutes."

It was obvious to everyone who met him that Ken was a special case. Why had it not been obvious to me?

My excuse is that the interview process had been a formality. It would have been tough — more like impossible — to say "no" to his arrival, and there was really no legitimate reason to do so under the circumstances. Ken had been pre-approved by the Board, and he was not just qualified on paper, but extremely well qualified — a near perfect fit for the position.

But the outcome of this short-circuited process was really more than that: I just did not know what to look for or how to interpret the many signals that by now should have been palpable.

The interview was a cordial affair. Maybe that's the way I wanted it. Push away any uneasiness. Don't look for something that you hope is not there.
Ken had walked in, and we shook hands. His stature was impressive. He was dressed immaculately and looked the part of a confident senior executive, although he seemed slightly ill at ease and was a little stiff. This would not change, and he would be as wooden when he left as when he arrived.

"I've reviewed your résumé, and I think you're going to enjoy working here," I began. "I'd like to hear anything else you might want to tell me about yourself, and then we can discuss the job and answer any questions you might have."

Ken shifted in his chair. He briefly walked me through his career. "I've had 120 senior people working for me for the last five years," and he laid out an impressive list of supervisory responsibilities that he held.

I thought from the way he framed his comments that he was suggesting this job would be a shadow of his previous one.

"You'll have fewer people working for you here," I had agreed, "but your position is very 'hands-on' for someone at your level. The scope of our activities has grown over the past several years, and the pace is intense. Your division produces all the academic materials for our courses, and you have personal oversight of both the content and the schedule. You'll find it's quite demanding, but perhaps in a different way than you're used to at your current position." I smiled and waited for a reply. Ken sat stone-faced.

"The research division falls under your scope as well, and Al and I were thinking of moving them out from under you and having the chief report directly to me. But given your experience and background, we'd like to leave them where they are."

"I have a lot of experience doing research," Ken replied, "and I'd like to keep that responsibility."

I told him that the research division was rapidly expanding its scope and reach, generating new visibility and requiring new relationships. Although it had a capable chief, I said, it would still require his attention.

"You'll discover that your job is important and central to our continued success, challenging and certainly interesting given your background," I concluded. Although Ken asked no questions, he appeared to be pleased.

He then recounted a story about a run-in that he had with his last boss because he felt his boss was spending too much time in his area. He made it sound like t was a trivial incident and cordially settled. Odd that he would have even mentioned it, I thought. A shot across the bow or was he preempting in case I talked to his old boss?

Next came Ken's explanation for why he did not get promoted out of his current position. I had noticed that he had been moving horizontally between organizations in the company for the last 10 years, but I also knew at his level that hitting a plateau was not necessarily unusual — or an indication of bad performance. The truth was that not everyone can be pushed to the top. I admit that the reasons he gave were only from his perspective, but I was not alarmed. After all, big egos were in play, and I had heard similar musings before.

What I did not know was that he made the short list for a job in another office that would have led to a promotion, but he had not been selected. Working for me was the only alternative — and it represented another unsatisfying lateral move.

This probably explained the unsolicited justification. "I didn't belong to the right clique," he said. "I wouldn't be a yes man," he asserted. I had not detected bitterness in his voice, and he seemed to have come to terms with his disappointment.

What I did rot realize was that this "acceptance" is part of a narcissist's personality disorder. *A narcissist never conducts a personal inventory or a self-examination that might question his own perspective.* He truly believes, even when the rest of the world is saying otherwise, that only he is right. Only his perspective counts. It would never occur to the narcissist that not getting promoted might have something to do with him. That failing to reach a higher level was his own doing, the result of his own actions.

And this was the theme that was common to everything Ken said during the interview: *None of the bad that has happened to me during my career was my fault.*

Had his hiring not been a done deal and had I done a normal interview, would I have detected this character flaw? I am not sure. Throughout the interview Ken expressed confidence and had a presence about him that was attractive.

We talked briefly about some of the other expectations of his position, and he seemed attentive and comfortable that he would be a good fit.

"I'm looking forward to coming to your office," he said. I characterized that remark as the result of reflection rather than inconsistent with what my personal assistant told me earlier.

We chatted a little more. I asked about his specific experience, but never threw him a probing question. It was surface stuff, the substance of an unremarkable conversation.

It did not occur to me when he asked me a few questions about my own experience and background that he might be sizing me up. He mentioned that he had 120 senior people under him in his last job, whereas I had only 30 senior people working for me. He also noted that he had been in the business his entire career, whereas I had been in and out of the business for only the last dozen years or so. He was seven years older than I was and had been a lecturer on the company's six-month course that I attended as a young executive more than a decade earlier. I never served at his level but had leapfrogged into my current position. The question about my Ph.D. I thought reflected sincere interest in why someone with a technical background would be working in a field where nearly everyone else, he included, was educated in the humanities.

Despite these points that I mention in retrospect, from my perspective our discussions were positive. All of us have our detractors, I had thought. "He has his obviously, and so do I." With that quick reflection as to why he might not have been as well liked at his last job as all of us would like to be, I put the rumors to rest.

"What did you think?" asked my personal assistant after Ken departed.

"Hard to tell," I said. "I think he'll be OK. He has lots of experience, and he's looking forward to joining us." I shrugged. "I'll ask Al what he thought."

"My friend called me again," she said, implying there was new information. I turned to listen. "You can't trust him."

I talked to Al later that afternoon. He would tell me that he also had been favorably impressed.

What is a Narcissist?

This next section gets technical, but I think it's important to know what the "experts" say about narcissism.

The *DSM-IV*, published by the American Psychiatric Association, is considered by many in the field as the psychologist's Bible. Revised in 2000, the new edition is designated the *DSM-IV-TR*. Another text, the *DSM-IV-TR Case Studies, A Clinical Guide to Differential Diagnosis* attempts to bring life to the descriptions and criteria outlined in the *DSM-IV-TR*. [1] It is in the *DSM*, as it's called by people in the business, that criteria are given that can be measured against a person's symptoms to determine if that person actually has a personality disorder, and it is the *Clinical Guide* that provides real life examples and discusses how to differentiate among the disorders that affect the human condition.

The *DSM* describes human personality traits as "enduring patterns of perceiving, relating to, and thinking about the environment and oneself that are exhibited in a wide range of social and personal contexts." To be considered a Personality Disorder, a person's personality traits must be inflexible and maladaptive, constitute an enduring pattern that is pervasive across a broad spectrum of personal and social situations, and lead to impairment or distress in social, occupational, or other important areas of

---

[1] Allen Frances, M.D. and Ruth Ross, M.A., *DSM-IV-TR Case Studies, A Clinical Guide to Differential Diagnosis* (American Psychiatric Publishing, Inc, London, England, 2001), p 277.

functioning.

My experience with Ken suggests that in the case of narcissism, personal and professional relationships become intertwined to such a degree that both the social and occupational lives of the narcissist are greatly affected.

The *DSM* goes on to tell us that a person with a Narcissistic Personality Disorder exhibits a pervasive pattern of grandiosity, the need for admiration and a lack of empathy for others. With Ken, the grandiosity was striking and in social situations was readily visible at the first introduction. His need for admiration was nearly constant and was reflected in behavior that was often disturbing. His lack of empathy usually first manifested itself in the context of a disagreement.

Narcissists also tend to exaggerate their accomplishments and talents, and they expect to be recognized as superior without commensurate achievements. This is particularly true when they have been appointed to an important position. Preoccupied with fantasies of unlimited success and brilliance, narcissists believe they are "special" and "unique" and should only associate with other special or high-status people. Ken "dropped names" of important people that he had met, mentioned important conferences to which he had been personally invited, and spoke of his extensive influence in the community. A decade earlier he was intimately involved in a significant milestone affecting the company, and he made reference to this event whenever the opportunity allowed.

Narcissists have unreasonable expectations of

especially favorable treatment or automatic compliance with their expectations. They tend to be arrogant, and they may take advantage of others to achieve their own ends.

A true narcissist is rare. The Mayo Clinic has a website that talks about the Narcissistic Personality Disorder, and it tells us that narcissists are more likely to be men than women.[2]

Many accomplished leaders like Ken have traits that can be characterized as narcissistic. They may be extremely ambitious, proud, shrewd and confident. I have known successful people who possess all these characteristics and flamboyance as well. But these characteristics were generally the result of a healthy self-esteem and a realistic appraisal of their capabilities. Effective leaders are also loyal to both their superiors and the people who work for them. I learned that narcissists, on the other hand, are loyal only to themselves.

In laymen's terms, narcissists have an inflated and generally unrealistic sense of their own importance, and a deep and abiding need for admiration. In cases like Ken's, narcissists tend to be intelligent, articulate and physically attractive people.
Ken consistently tried to gain the attention of others, pontificating at conferences and meetings alike. The discussions at times seemed interminable because he was compelled to ask long questions of our guests and offer his "well-founded" opinion on every

---

[2] See "Narcissistic Personality Disorder" at *mayoclinic.com/health/narcissistic-personality-disorder*, 27 April 2008.

topic. Ken had a seemingly insatiable need to be "on the podium" and speaking in front of a group, where he could showcase his talents. I remember thinking after watching one of his "performances" that the experience had transformed him, similar to the effects of alcohol or a "fix".

When given the opportunity, Ken scheduled himself to be the first speaker at a conference or made arrangements to ensure a prominent role — often ignoring and bypassing protocol. When confronted, he had an innocuous reason prepared to explain away any self-serving motivation on his part for his actions.

A book written to tell us why we love, feel and act the way we do, informs us that narcissists do not just believe that they are superior to others — they openly display their sense of superiority and in turn show little regard for other people's feelings.[3] It is this sense of self-importance and superiority, while at the same time feeling justified in having so little respect for others that permits the narcissist to behave in ways that a normal person is not prepared to fathom or can even begin to anticipate.

The startling combination of self-love and malice for others is the narcissist's hallmark.

Unashamed arrogance and over-confidence are what the casual observer sees on the outside, but the

---

[3] Dr Tim Clinton and Dr Gary Sibcy, *Attachments — Why You Love, Feel and Act the Way You Do*, (Integrity Publishers, Brentwood, Tennessee, 2002), pp 68-69.

reality underneath is actually quite different. The narcissist lacks self confidence and is vulnerable to even the slightest criticism.

Because a narcissist cannot sustain a persistent and stable self-image, he depends on the praise of others as a barometer of his self-esteem.[4] The value of coworkers is determined by how they contribute to the narcissist's view of himself, and when a coworker does not give him the kind of positive feedback a narcissist believes he is entitled to, he may become impatient or angry. In Ken's case, this led to unexpected responses when there was disagreement and overreactions to innocent comments or healthy criticism.

When under stress, the narcissist becomes combative and contemptuous. His pride swells, his defense system punches into overdrive, and he counterattacks his critics for having the gall to confront him.

The narcissist may be unwilling, even incapable of hearing what others say. The narcissist is openly jealous of others' success and is sure that he could — and should — be doing his boss' job.

There is no definitive cause of narcissism, and narcissists do not necessarily share a common past. Although its onset may be traced back to adolescence or early adulthood, it is unclear when narcissism begins and how it eventually grows to encompass a personality. Researchers claim to be

---

[4]   See "Narcissistic Personality Disorder" at *cnn.com/health/library*.

learning more, but symptoms are the only evidence of the disorder, and answers as to why they appear are elusive. You can look at the references I have cited if you'd like to explore the "risk factors" in greater deta l.

My experience with Ken taught me that the narcissist will ultimately have conflict at work because he is unable to separate his professional life from his personal one. This has profound implications.

The narcissist has one world, and he resides in the middle of t. There stands the narcissist on a pedestal, and from his perspective everyone else — friends, family, coworkers — are situated all around always facir g in his direction. The consequence is that every situation — no matter whether the narcissist is directly involved or not — is personalized. That's why no matter the conversation, the narcissist eventually makes the conversation about himself. That's also why professional differences become personal disagreements.

Every professional setback or decision he does not agree with affects the narcissist's self-esteem. It surprises his coworkers at the intensity of dislike the narcissist develops for those around him who may not share his perspective or judgment.

Conflict at work is likely to happen early in his tenure. This was certainly true in Ken's case. The challenge is to recognize the narcissist and for supervisors to agree that something needs to be done.

It is this moment of "discovery" when either the narcissist is removed from the workplace by those in charge, or he begins systematically to undermine his coworkers, his superiors and the organization. It is at this moment that the leadership must recognize that there is nothing positive a narcissist can bring to an organization that would overcome the damage he will inflict. This moment, quite literally, is the moment of truth.

Sadly, few leaders and even fewer managers are prepared to deal with a narcissist and take appropriate action. After all, it is the American way to make things work and get along with people, especially in high performing organizations.

Legal constraints may also be a factor when it comes to removing an employee, as corporate lawyers are hesitant to take action against even problematic individuals without evidence of wrongdoing — and usually lots of it. The advantage of taking action as soon as the narcissist is recognized is that the less time he has spent in the office the easier it is to justify removal.

If allowed to remain in his position, in the best of circumstances the narcissist becomes deeply entrenched and is typically marginalized and tolerated until an excuse can be found to move him to another job — the old body shuffle. Removing him is just too hard and painful.

That's why he ends up in your office. Or in this case, mine.

In the worst of circumstances, the narcissist tries to tarnish the reputation of his superiors, continuously creates upheaval that affects the morale of his coworkers, drives others from the workplace, and ultimately weakens the organization.

Because he is so self-centered, a narcissist's actions and decisions almost always reflect his own personal agenda rather than what will benefit others or the organization. This frequently leads to the narcissist exercising poor judgment and indulging in unethical practices, a certain recipe for conflict.

CHAPTER TWO

Assumptions Make an *Ass* out of *u* and *me*

During the middle of our six-month course for up-and-coming managers, we sent the participants on a three-week tour to various locations across the company to hear from and meet with prominent personalities in our business. They were accompanied by members of the staff who had already successfully completed the program, along with a pair of executives selected from our office.

We designated a staff member to coordinate the program and accompany the group while on tour. The program had existed for decades because of its high regard by both participants and hosts, and the protocol was well established.

While on tour, the days were filled with stimulating lectures on current events and topics relevant to our business. The evenings were filled with dinners and receptions where participants could mingle with people they would rarely meet socially otherwise. The staff members who went along guided the group and led vigorous question and answer periods that were planned after each presentation. The participants used these sessions to explore issues in more depth or to raise related topics the speakers may not have covered. The executives from our office who accompanied the tour provided a presence, met with their counterparts at each location, and gave appropriate remarks to the hosts to reflect the group's gratitude for their hospitality.

The "tradition" of the staff members leading the question and answer session after each presentation became nearly as important for them as the program was for the participants. It was a chance for them to stand up in front of the company's senior executives and to develop and strengthen relationships. The division of labor for the conduct of the Q&A was carefully planned by the staff prior to the tour, and it was a highlight of their activities.

Al and I agreed that Dick, the Director of human resources and the service support side of the business, and Ken should accompany the group. Even though neither one had done the tour, we had confidence in our longtime tour guide and knew that he would be handling the details and directing the activities. Furthermore, the staff met prior to departure to plan out the detailed choreography for the entire period of travel.

Ken told a group of us that he was never allowed to go on the six-month course because his boss did not think there was anything that he could learn from it. The comment should have given Al and me pause — not just the part that there was nothing Ken could learn, although I was already wondering whether Ken was teachable — but because his boss refused to send him.

But Al and I were not worried. The tour itself was a well-oiled machine. Soldier proof. Idiot proof. All the clichés applied.

Nothing could go wrong.

When Symptoms Appear — The First Warning Signs

Right away Ken's behavior was remarkable.

He was incapable of walking into a session or meeting without "announcing" his arrival. Invariably his shoes clicked loudly on the floor and echoed throughout the room when he entered, and he slammed the door behind him when he walked into meetings. He had a tendency to arrive late, and since he typically sat in a reserved place where he was visible, he could not be ignored. He seemed powerless to sit quietly and usually plopped into his chair. He would throw open his notebook and noisily flip through the pages as he grandly pulled a pen out to write with. He crossed and uncrossed his legs incessantly, and he slapped his feet on the floor with loud "claps" each time he changed posture.

During guest lectures in the auditorium, Ken sat in the front row and engaged others in conversation. This was particularly true when he sat next to visitors. He seemed oblivious to the fact that his *tête-à-tête* was not only distracting but rude.

When important guests were in the audience, protocol put Ken far to the left. But when the session ended, Ken hurriedly placed himself so that he could "meet" our visitors as they left the auditorium. We typically took pictures to record visits, and Ken would engage the VIPs in conversation until we arrived where the photo would be taken. He habitually ended up standing in the center of the front row for the picture, and Al and I would have to push him aside to respect protocol.

During meetings it was not unusual for Ken to look at his watch repeatedly to show his impatience when others talked. He often brought in reams of paper to work on, ignoring the proceedings until he was required to provide input or decided that something interested him.

Ken's lack of courtesy was so unexpected coming from a senior executive with his experience that I was sure it was atypical and would end with the negative attention t brought from everyone around him.

I of course was unaware that narcissists thrive on attention, negative or otherwise. Unlike flamboyant personalities who may try to "make a statement" with their grand entrance, narcissists believe that special people are always noticed, always being watched. And since the narcissist believes that he is special, Ken felt that he should always be noticed, too — regardless of the impression his behavior made on others. I would also learn that if circumstances are calm for too long a period and the narcissist feels ignored, he will generate controversy or conflict whose sole benefit is to turn everyone's attention to him.

Warning Signs Turn to Danger Signals

It was whie Ken was away on the tour that I happened to talk to his assistant manager.

"I can't do my job." The sentence seemed to burst out when I asked Lenny casually how things were going.

"What do you mean?" I asked, surprised by his

response. Lenny was one of the most reliable and productive employees we had, and this was the first time I ever heard him complain about anything.

"Ken's never here. He's always traveling. He expects me to do his job for him, and I can't get to my own stuff. I'm drowning."

I had already talked to Ken about his excessive travel back to his old office. He was often absent, and I found myself sending emails that he could read upon his return when it would have been easier to have a short conversation. This comment from Lenny was confirmation that Ken had not responded to my observation that his absences were becoming an issue not just for me, but for his people, too.

"I'll talk to him when he gets back," I promised. "How's everything else going?"

"OK." He sounded relieved that he had been able to raise the subject with me.

"Keep me posted on how you're doing, will you?" I wanted to know whether things would improve without sounding like I was checking up on Ken.

"Sure," he said.

A week after he returned from the tour, Ken was still missing because he flew to his old office immediately upon getting back. I looked into his travel arrangements and discovered that along with ongoing medical problems that were keeping him out of the office, he had been gone nearly two thirds of the time since he "arrived".

I went to Al and told him what Lenny said and that I would be talking to Ken about his frequent forays back home.

"He hasn't made the move to our office," I said. "I've asked him twice to reduce his travel. I'm going to ask him again and may have to ask you to intervene if he keeps it up." I did not have control over Ken's travel funds. Each executive had his own budget, and I wanted to alert my boss that he might have to step in. He agreed.

Little did I know that my concern about his frequent flying would become a mere addendum to a much longer discussion.

The next day Tim, one of Lenny's colleagues, came into my office.

"I need to talk to you," he said, and he closed the door. This was the first time Tim had come to my office without an appointment, and I invited him to sit down.

"Hank came to talk to me about what Ken did while they were together on the tour. He didn't want to come to you directly, and he did not want me to talk to you, either. But I think I need to inform you."

"OK," I said.

Tim was a member of the combined staff, and I did not know him that well. I did know that he and Hank were friends, because as staff members they shared similar responsibilities. I would get to know Tim much better over the course of the next year.

"When the Q&A came up the first time, instead of letting the staff lead the discussion, Ken took over."

"Why would he do that?" I wondered aloud. "Did Wally talk to him about our policies?" (Wally was the tour coordinator.)

Tim shrugged. "I imagine he did, but I don't know for sure. Hank said when his turn came up to lead the Q&A, he took the podium only to have Ken shove him off the stage. He was embarrassed."

I shook my head. It was only one of many times that Ken would be oblivious to the effect his behavior had on others.

"Something else, too," he went on.

I sat back and crossed my arms.

"Apparently Hank was riding with Ken and another executive in a limo on the way from the hotel to a presentation, and Hank said something that contradicted Ken. He said that Ken turned to him in the back seat and angrily asked, 'What are you doing riding with us, anyway? Shouldn't you be on the buses with everyone else?' Hank was friends with the other executive, and he was mortified."

I shook my head again. "I'll talk to Wally first and then I'll go to Hank. Thanks for coming by to let me know."

I called Wally at home.

"Hey, Wally, I heard that Ken led all the Q&A sessions while you guys were on tour. Did you tell him that wasn't his job? That the accompanying staff members were supposed to lead the discussions after each presentation?"

"Yes, of course, but he insisted that he was going to do it, anyway."

"Why didn't you call me?" I asked.

"Well, I think that Ken asked the team if anyone objected to his leading the Q&A."

"What did he expect the team to say? He's a senior executive. It was inappropriate for him to even ask the question — to put his people on the spot like that. You should have been more assertive, Wally."

Wally got defensive. "I tried to tell him the next day again, but he wouldn't listen. He told me that everyone was comfortable with his leading the discussions and that he wasn't interested in my opinion anymore."

"OK, I appreciate the situation you were in. I'm just having difficulty understanding why this would even happen. Next time I expect a phone call." I hung up in frustration. I went to the office of one of the other staff members who had gone on the tour with Hank.

"Carol, I spoke with Wally just now about the tour, and he said that Ken led all the discussions. Can you tell me what happened?"

She worked directly for Ken and was hesitant to reply. "Well, after the first morning Wally told Ken that we were supposed to be leading the Q&A. So Ken called all of us together and asked if we had any objections to his leading the discussions."

"And?" I asked after a long pause.

"Well, what did you expect me to say? He's my boss. No one said anything and neither did I, so Ken led all the discussions."

"For the entire tour?"

Carol nodded.

I went to Hank's office.

"Do you have a second?" I asked.

Hank was uncomfortable but relieved that I had come to talk to him. He proceeded to relay the same stories, and was particularly upset about the incident in the car with Ken and his former supervisor.

I went to Al and told him what happened.

"I'll be talking to him about this when he gets back from his trip," I said.

But that wasn't the end of it. I no sooner returned to my office when an old friend and mentor I had worked for in the past called me. He served in my position previously and was retired, but he still showed up whenever the tour came to his part of town.

"Who's this Ken guy?" he asked.

"He's our new hire," I said. "He replaced Greg. Why do you ask?" I was not sure I wanted to hear his answer.

"What's his problem?"

"I don't know what you mean."

"He was talking to a big group of us at a dinner reception. Didn't know who any of us were. But he told us that you weren't qualified for your job. Said that you didn't have the right education. He said that he should be the Director of the academic program, or at the very least should be working directly for Al and not for you."

I was surprised and admittedly confused.

"What made me the topic of conversation?"

"I asked him who he was and whether he knew you. He took it from there. Once he started, he just kept talking. Didn't give anyone else a chance to say anything. I finally walked away."

"I've been told that he did some other strange stuff on the tour, too, and I was already planning to talk to him." I was shaking my head. "This seems to be one more indication that he may not be a good fit for our office," I thought out loud.

"By the way," my friend said. "I really liked Dick. A good guy and much better than his predecessor."

"I like him, too," I said. We ended the conversation with a few more niceties.

As a final data point, I went and spoke with Dick. "How did Ken do on the trip?"

"Fine." He told me that he had no problems with Ken.

Only later would Dick reveal that he did have problems. And Ken would treat Dick so disrespectfully during their second tour together that upon their subsequent return Dick said he'd never travel with Ken again.

I went into Al's office. "You're not going to believe this."

The Folly of Confrontation

I gave Ken a couple days to catch up and then asked him to come to my office.

I skipped the small talk. "I'd like to talk to you about a couple issues that came up while you were on the tour."

Ken's body language changed from relaxed to tense, and he got a look on his face that was to become a familiar one: a scowl that expressed extreme displeasure.

"The first thing I'd like to talk about is the tour itself. I spoke to Wally about how it went, and he said that you unilaterally made the decision to lead all the Q&A sessions. I was wondering why you decided to take on that role and then ignored Wally when he tried to discuss the issue with you."

"Did he say I did a bad job?"

"You're missing the point. Even if you did a great job, leading the Q&A wasn't your role."

"I received compliments from everyone on the way I led the discussions."

I looked at him, really I think, for the first time. "I'm sure you did a great job, Ken. But again, that's not the issue here. Our tradition is that the staff accompanying the tour leads the Q&A. Wally told you that, and you decided to ignore him. Maybe you can try to help me understand exactly what happened."

"Well," he said, "when the first presentation ended, no one stood up to lead the Q&A. So I decided to do something about it and took charge."

"Did you really think that no one was prepared to lead the discussions? That you had to leap up and save the day? We've been doing this for decades. Why would you think that no one was prepared to lead the Q&A?"

"Well, it looked to me like no one was reacting."

"OK, let's say that happened. But why did you keep leading the discussions after Wally told you the staff was supposed to lead them?"

"After Wally talked to me, I called all the staff together and asked if they had any objections to my doing all the Q&A, and no one had a problem with it."

"Did you really expect that anyone would take issue with you?" I asked. "Of course they're not going to say anything if you insisted. Why would you think otherwise?"

Ken shrugged. "Did you talk to Dick?"

"In fact I did," I replied.

"Did he say that I did a good job leading the Q&A or not?"

I was dumbstruck.

"Even if he did, it's immaterial to this discussion." I paused and took another hard look at Ken. He seemed unable to engage in a logical conversation. "I'm just very surprised that when Wally talked to you that you ignored him. It's a tradition that the staff leads the Q&A. It's their opportunity to stand up in front of their peers and our colleagues. You and I don't need that chance."

Ken remained expressionless, his face an enigma.

"It wasn't your job to lead the Q&A on the tour. Your role was to provide a presence. To represent our office." No response.

"I'd also like to talk to you about what happened between you and Hank while riding in the car."

Ken denied the incident ever happened.

"It never happened?"

"I don't remember it," he claimed.

I thought he was lying, not yet attributing events that were happening to a personality disorder. Narcissists, it seems, cannot remember their outbursts. This was the first of numerous outbursts that Ken would make in front of others and would be unable to recall when confronted.

"I'd like to switch gears and talk about your role as our representative while you're on the tour. I got a call the other day from an old friend. He said when he was talking to you at a reception that you announced to the entire group that I didn't have the right qualifications to do my job. That in fact your background made you more qualified than me and that you should be the Director of academics for the six-month course."

The look on his face betrayed his surprise. "Who told you that?"

"What difference does it make who told me?" I asked.

"I was only kidding when I said it. I wasn't serious."

"If you were only kidding," I answered, "then why would you say such a thing? You're supposed to represent our office. Why would you criticize me or anyone else, for that matter? What was the point? What was your motivation?"

Ken shrugged. "If you had been there, you would have known that I wasn't making a serious comment."

"I still don't understand why you made the comment in the first place."

Ken could not give an answer to my question.

"I'd like to talk about one more thing: travel. You need to move to our office."
He looked perplexed. "What do you mean I need to move? I am here."

"You may be present now, but you're spending more time at your last office than your new one."

The scowl returned.

"You're not doing your job. You're relying too much on your people. You need to be present."

Again, Ken did not engage in conversation.

I finally said, "I want you to stop traveling." But without control over his travel budget, I was making a demand I could not enforce.

I called my old boss after Ken left the office. "I talked to Ken about what he said at the reception, and he said he was only kidding when he made the comments about me."

There was a laugh at the other end. "He didn't sound like he was kidding. He was very clear that he was too well qualified to be working for someone like you."

Later that afternoon, Dick made a point to stop me in the hall.

"I wanted to tell you that Ken did a good job leading the Q&A during the tour." He smiled uncomfortably.

"So I heard," I replied.

An Inability to Cooperate

Al held an extended meeting with the senior staff once a week. It was painful, but he viewed it as a necessity. It was his way of having direct interaction with the key people in the office and keeping us all apprised of his thinking and where he thought the organization should be going. Many times he presented new ideas and changes that he wanted to make through our various efforts. It was also an opportunity for the rest of us to raise new proposals and have the staff react to them.

Although I'm not a fan of long meetings, I supported Al's prerogative to hold them. He went over all the activities that were on the calendar. He religiously covered in detail each activity and asked questions. "What's the status? When will I have this document? What should I be briefing to the Board? Who's writing my remarks? What are we planning to say and emphasize? What do you guys think?"

We never set deadlines. There was a running list of action items that were talked about, and as progress was made they were updated and eventually closed. This *laissez faire* process worked until Ken arrived. It seemed that Ken was incapable of making progress on the action items for which he was responsible. No amount of cajoling on Al's part made a difference.

I was glad for this development, because I attributed most of the problem to Ken's frequent travel. When Ken was absent and his number two or three was representing him at the table, it was clear that neither one of them had any clue about any of the action items — even those that affected them and their divisions.

When Ken missed another of Al's meetings and more deadlines were dropped because he was on travel, Al finally called him to his office and ordered him to stop traveling.

"I'll personally approve all trips you make from now on," he told Ken. This was the fifth time Ken had been confronted about his frequent travel, and it took direct intervention from the top man to get him to agree to change his behavior.

But Al's direct intervention would only work for awhile. It was normal and rational for Al to expect that a subordinate would comply with his direction and not require further guidance, but Ken was not normal — or rational.

Once Ken discovered that he could get away with ignoring Al's direction, he became an animal unleashed. He seemed to possess a well honed instinct for pulling back just enough to avoid provoking Al. The fallout, though, was that Ken refused to conform with guidance from either Al or me unless one of us explicitly confronted him and demanded compliance.

Ken's refusal to work constructively with others would eventually create almost constant friction between us. I have to admit that I grew weary of the conflict and began sending emails rather than talking to Ken personally. I had held my own bi-weekly meetings to cover academic issues, but I tired of his excuses and stonewalling and what I considered unprofessional behavior. Rightly or wrongly, I discontinued my regular meetings and only called them when there was something important to discuss. I learned quickly that direct confrontation on any issue was unproductive and that Ken's promises to meet timelines or provide material were meaningless. I decided that I needed to put my expectations in writing and when I followed up emails with additional correspondence, I attached the earlier documentation to make the point that we had already discussed the issue without any results.

Ken held a key pos tion, and the effectiveness of my part of the organization was tied directly to his performance. I found myself preparing daily for battle to get Ken to do what was expected. Because of the growing conf ict between us, Ken began taking his frustration out cn his people, and I began to hear that his criticism of me in his staff meetings had become both relentless and ruthless. If I suggested that he stop criticizing me in front of others, he denied any wrongcoing and demanded to know who had said he was being critical.

The misery of his people — one of the staff members came to me and expressed his distress about the situation — led me to retreat, and I found myself choosing my battles carefully. I began to feel like I was dealing with a rebellious child.

Al would later make a similar comment in response to Ken's demand that he quit treating him like a teenager. "Then quit acting like one!" Al finally bellowed.

I would ultimately get Al to agree to organizational and process changes that reduced Ken's ability to thwart my side of the organization and in turn the need for frequen∶ confrontation. While this was effective, Ken knew that he was being marginalized, which increased his anger and the intensity of his criticism of both Al and me in front of others.

We also decided to impose deadlines on each action item that came out of Al's meetings. The assistant who took notes had taken to sending out emails reminding us that certain items were due, but that did not work. Setting a firm deadline while everyone was present was the only way to draw Ken's attention to the fact that he was ignoring his responsibilities, and it gave Al the leverage he needed to get Ken moving on an issue. Criticizing him openly in front of the entire staff for not meeting a deadline worked most of the time.

People affected by Ken's inaction would usually come to me asking if I would make a decision in place of Ken. If Ken was gone on travel, I told Lenny to make a decision. If Ken was present, I would raise the issue at Al's meeting. When deadlines became critical, I told people to "just go ahead and do what you think needs to be done."

Ken would often make a statement in our meetings that he was on top of an issue, but when the time came for action nothing happened.

We had a vice president from another company coming to town to talk about a joint venture. His office had called asking if he could drop by for a visit as part of preliminary discussions. I was the one who decided that a visit would be a good idea, but Ken was responsible for handing out the formal invitation. I heard from the VP's office that the invitation had never been received, and when I raised the issue at Al's meetings Ken assured us that he was taking care of it. He never did.

By the time the protocol office asked me to intervene personally, the VP felt so disrespected that he said he no longer had time to come by. We were grossly embarrassed, and I vowed never to allow Ken's inaction to damage our reputation again.

For this vow I would pay a hefty price.

Revenge

Since Hank's run-in with Ken, in Ken's eyes Hank was *persona non grata*.

A key job was opening up in Ken's division, and Al and I decided that Hank was the right guy. Ken insisted otherwise.

Both Al and I on separate occasions told Ken that we thought Hank should get the nod. Ken's response was to go to Hank and tell him that he was not qualified for the new position and that he would be choosing Bob.

I was upset and spoke to Ken. "Why would you tell Hank that he isn't qualified when both Al and I told you that we don't agree with your assessment?"

I told Hank that we did not agree with what Ken had said, but the damage was done. Furthermore, Al would not insist on Hank's being assigned to the new position. Instead, he seemed determined to convince Ken that Hank should get the job.

But Ken dug in. He wrote a very long epistle on why Bob was more qualified, ignoring what Al and I had laid out in support of Hank.

Known to us only after the fact, Ken also began antagonizing Hank at every opportunity. It finally ended with Hank stomping out of his own office with Ken present. Ken ostensibly wanted to talk to Hank and refused to leave when Hank felt the conversation was getting ugly.

Hank came to both Al and me and said that he could not work for Ken and wanted to be put in a different division. Dick, who ran human resources, said that he could not assign Hank to Ken, despite Al's and my recommendation, given all the turmoil. Al reluctantly agreed.

Hank's attitude and morale spiraled into the toilet, and he became completely unproductive until finally leaving a year later.

And Hank wasn't the only victim. Sue came to me just before the New Year.

"I'm going to file a grievance with human resources against Ken."

"Why, what happened?"

"He's heavy-handed and a bully. He treats me disrespectfully. I don't have to take that kind of disrespect from anybody."

"Have you talked to him about your feelings?"

She admitted she had not.

"Why don't you talk to Ken first? If his response doesn't make you happy, then come back to me and let me know that you intend to go to HR. You have my full support in whatever decision you make."

Sue went to Ken and was candid about her feelings. He apologized, and she was satisfied.

I know that I made the right management decision in how I handled that particular situation, but in retrospect it was one of at least three opportunities where I could have elevated Ken's disrespectful behavior toward others. Instead, I defused the complaints each time. Was that a mistake? A missed opportunity? Would it have been unethical to use the situation with Sue as a lever to expose Ken's misconduct?

I told Al about Sue's run-in with Ken so that if she changed her mind and went to HR, he would not be blindsided.

But even Ken had survival instincts. He knew that he could antagonize a male coworker, but with women there was an underlying assumption of sexual harassment that could be lethal. As this was a potentially fatal situation, he backed off. I checked with Sue a number of times after the incident, and she said that Ken had completely changed his demeanor and interaction with her.

Ken fawned over the secretaries who worked for him. With responsibility for creating and executing a significant flow of material, he had more secretaries than anyone else. He asked for promotions his secretaries did not deserve nor were eligible for and claimed that his people worked harder than anyone else in the organization. He prohibited the members of the staff working for him from taking on anything that he did not personally assign. When I tried to offer extra projects to his people, Ken emphatically said "no".

Ken protested the office reorganization I worked with Al, which included the movement of the research division so that its director reported to me. While protesting loudly, in the very next breath he claimed he had neither the time nor the resources to meet the schedules demanded to do his job.

This mantra of "too much work for the people I have" would become his way of parrying criticism directed at him for failing to meet agreed timelines.

I viewed Ken's attitude as a positive when I tired of the confrontation, in that it gave me an opening to avoid giving Ken projects that had short deadlines.

I began to feel like a manipulative bureaucrat.

Ken continued to castigate Al and me in front of his team. This was extremely upsetting to Ben, one of our most respected staff members, and he told Ken directly that he viewed his conduct as unprofessional. But Ken would not relent. In fact, Ken eventually took to criticizing both of us openly in front of anyone who would listen. Ben finally refused to attend Ken's staff meetings.

"Ken is the most unprofessional senior executive I have ever met," Ben said to me before resigning a year before his contract was due to end. We could not change Ben's mind. Ben had also spoken to Al on numerous occasions about Ken, hoping that Al would put an end to Ken's bad behavior. One of our biggest stars, Ben's loss was devastating to the office.

One outsider who was doing collaborative work with our office knew Ken well from a previous project. "I'll only work with you if Ken is not my point of contact. Otherwise, my office won't do business with yours. Ken is impossible to work with."

I came to know the company drivers quite well during my tenure, heading across the city once or twice a week. It was while one of the young drivers was taking me to my destination that he volunteered, "Ken is bad news. None of us wants to drive him anywhere." I had not mentioned Ken. I did not have to. He was wreaking havoc with everyone.

Al and I took a chance meeting with a former Board Member and boss of Ken's to ask about him. He crossed his arms and spent the next two hours telling us things we wished we had never heard.

"I personally pulled the plug on his career and made sure he was never promoted again," he said. "Ken can't take any constructive criticism, and he always has a personal agenda that does not reflect the best interests of the company. He often takes credit for the work of others and exaggerates his own contributions."

"So why is he still working for the company? Why hasn't he been fired?" I decided to be more direct. "Why didn't you fire him?"

"It's too hard. He's got a lot of support from several members of the Board. I did what I could, blocking any move that would have led to a promotion."

He would later use a metaphor to describe Ken that I would never forget.

"Ken is like an old codger who takes the wrong highway onramp in the dead of night and starts driving against traffic on the wrong side of the highway. Every time he passes a driver going in the right direction, he wonders where all the idiots are coming from."

My wife came to me and mentioned that the other wives in the office were talking to her about the lack of respect their husbands were developing for Al because Ken's misconduct was tolerated. The culmination of his early bad behavior was Ken's humiliation of his wife in public at one of our social activities. She had gone off to help one of the wives on the six-month course, leaving him alone in a group of VIPs. He scolded her like a child in front of everyone when she returned. She was reduced to tears and in the ladies' bathroom confided that "I don't know if I can stay with my husband anymore. He is so abusive."

I knew exactly what she meant.

Time to Act

Seven months had passed since Ken arrived, and I had enough.

I went to Al.

"Al, Ken isn't working out. I have put together a list for you of what Ken has done since his arrival, and none of it is positive. I predict it will get worse. He needs to go. You've got to go to the Board and make a case." Since Ken was a senior executive, Al could not just fire him.

This was the moment of truth.

Ken had fully revealed his hand. My wife pegged him as a narcissist, and upon reading the literature and book passages written by clinical psychologists, I was easily convinced. It also made clear what we were up against.

Ken would never change. He was incapable of change. If anything, his mental disorder would only intensify.

"Al, Ken is a narcissist." I gave him a copy of literature describing the personality traits of a narcissist and briefly explained what that meant and its implications.

"There was something in the newspaper I read that essentially says you're better off leaving your job if the management at your organization won't take action against people like Ken. Ken's unprofessional behavior is a reflection of our lack of leadership. You've got to do something."

Al only nodded. "I know he's difficult. I'll make some inquiries."

Al gave no indication that he intended to take my recommendation, but I felt that I needed to prod him to make him aware of the harm that Ken was causing. I also wanted Ken's actions documented in his performance report. To that Al would not agree.

Apart from the personal criticism of Al by Ken in front of his people, Al had been mostly shielded from Ken's antics. I was taking the brunt of his abuse, and I was weary of it. I was beginning to wonder if the nearly constant flow of adrenaline I was feeling at work might eventually affect my health. For the very first time in my life, I was losing sleep.

When a few weeks later Al told me that he could not do anything — it would be too controversial — it changed our relationship. We had worked together for just over a year, and we were a good team. We had been a great team before Ken became a part of it. In a way I felt betrayed. Al seemed more worried about how he would be perceived by the Board if he took my recommendation than he was about how I, and everyone else for that matter, was being affected by Ken's actions.

When Al asked me to extend my contract, I only pursued the extension halfheartedly. My wife was angry that I would let Ken force me out as she put it, but the reality was that Ken was out of control, and I could do nothing about it.

Ultimately Al and I and our wives became close friends, but unfortunately too much of our conversation and energies would center on the misery generated by Ken's nearly constant obstreperous behavior.

What we did not know was that we had seen nothing yet.

CHAPTER THREE

From Bad to Worse

Ken's travel was limited to office-related business, but this still did not keep him from trying to travel. One of Al's colleagues called him saying that Ken had asked to be invited to come speak to his organization, and he wanted to know what Al thought of the idea. Al, annoyed at this end run, nixed it.

With his addiction to excessive traveling finally cured, Ken was now present almost full time at the office. He still did not know his job, and things continued to fall through the cracks. Lenny tried his best to make up for Ken's shortcomings, and Al began at the weekly meetings to hold Ken accountable for all the misfires that were regularly coming out of his division.

Lenny was being transferred to another office, and in the midst of the transition and Ken's lack of management, he was working well beyond his limits. He came in each morning before I did, and he was leaving late. Meanwhile, Ken was not putting in the hours nor devoting the attention that his position required, and he continued to fall farther behind.

Al had to give an important speech, and Lenny wrote a really good talk for him a few months earlier. So it was only natural that Al would ask Lenny to write this next one. Lenny was clearly overwhelmed as a result of the request. Reluctant to tell Al that he did not have the time, he put something together. He finished it just as Al was flying out to his conference, and on the plane Al reviewed it only to discover that the majority was an almost word by word rehash of what the CEO had recently said. Given that his audience would likely be familiar with the CEO's recent remarks, Al was furious. In his mind Lenny nearly caused a shipwreck.

Al was forced to write his own speech. When he returned, he let Lenny know that he was disappointed. What Al did not seem to appreciate was the pressure that Lenny was under because he was not only preparing to move while still doing his own fulltime job, but he was carrying a significant part of Ken's workload, too.

Ken had no email skills and could not keep up with the traffic. Hence he was out of the loop on nearly everything. He began to rail against technology and insisted at every opportunity that it was overrated and overused. Because I had instituted numerous technology changes for the office since my arrival and was always pushing for more, it was another way for him to put us at odds.

"Email should not replace face to face interaction between people," Ken said emphatically one day. "Management by email does not work."

In a way, I suppose Ken was right. But one big problem was that no one wanted face to face interaction with Ken unless it was in the context of a group or at a mandatory meeting.

Ken spoke only in monologue and specialized in arguing in support of the *status quo*. He dominated every conversation by telling stories — about himself. He was often overcome by events because he could not make timely decisions. He had grown stale. Any presentations that he prepared were reworks of briefings prepared by others — briefings that he would present elsewhere as if he were the author of the ideas.

A second problem was that the organizational hierarchy was relatively flat, and the scope of our responsibilities was significant. Things moved fast in our office, and asynchronous communication via email was the most effective way to conduct business with everyone always on the move. The experience and quality of our senior people in my view also meant that they did not require "management".

I called the combined staff together at the end of each six-month course for a day, and once a week I tried to touch base with each of them informally. I discovered that I got more feedback from a casual conversation in the hall or in the lunch room than I did from any formal interaction.

And finally, my relationship with Ken was just plain broken. He had taken to opposing outright every initiative that I proposed. As he was often responsible for making change possible, unless Al wanted my proposal to be implemented and insisted that Ken do it, nothing would happen.

Ken also began practicing what I characterized as malicious bureaucratic behavior. I had worked in high performing organizations for my entire career, and I never experienced the kinds of delaying tactics that Ken was using.

Ken "invented" so many actions seemingly designed

to undermine the organization and upper management that I had trouble determining whether what he did was subconscious or done on purpose. Perhaps it did not matter, as in the end it had the same effect.

I concluded that Ken's personality disorder was so deeply entrenched and that although he was aware of what he was doing, he was unable to grasp the broader consequences of what his actions in turn said about himself.

Friends and Enemies

In Ken's mind there were two kinds of people in the world: those who supported his views and catered unequivocally to his ego, and "the enemy".

Ken's wife was the former. She had learned to give Ken the positive feedback he so desperately needed. I am not certain that he returned the favor. His wife seemed constantly flustered and always on the verge of an anxiety attack.

Ken was the consummate "pencil pusher". He knew how to "play the system" when it came to people and resources. He continuously complained that he did not have enough people to do the work under his purview.

In contrast his counterpart, Ned, who executed the six-month course and competed with Ken for resources, always tried to do what was in the best interests of the office. Ken was quick to take advantage of Ned's goodwill. While giving the appearance of working with Ned, Ken never failed to make his case and suggest that Ned's division had a less important role than his own and hence deserved less priority when it came to allocating people and the necessary supporting resources.

The people under Ken over time became completely kowtowed. They spent most of the time in their offices, rarely venturing out. Much to my disappointment, his people mostly avoided me to avoid conflict with Ken. In Ken's world, they could not be "nice" to the boss and still be considered loyal employees to their supervisor.

The weight of this truth was revealed one Monday morning when I came to work and was greeted by Ken's people with smiles and friendly "hellos" that had been missing from the office for months. I cheerily returned their greetings and when I got to my desk I wondered about the change. Had something happened over the weekend? Was today a special day? Was there something going on this week that I forgot? Then it hit me. Ken was on travel. His people were free to be themselves.

I observed throughout the office that people from all the divisions were more relaxed, laughing more loudly and enjoying conversation in a way that once had been common. I remarked on the change to Al.

"The atmosphere is completely different with Ken gone."

But Al had already noticed, and this was the beginning of a realization on his part that Ken had indeed changed the dynamics of the organization.

And not of just any organization, but his.

Creating Discontent

Ken was particularly adept at identifying and allying himself with people in the office who were unhappy. While there were not many, he was swift to empathize with them and let them know that they had reason to be dissatisfied with the "incompetent leadership".

Ken cultivated relationships with the key staff that worked in Ned's division. To them he was especially cordial, and I learned that he used their conversations to talk about the conflict between himself and me. He intimated that "I was the one with the problem" and the instigator of disagreement. They seemed to agree with him. These were people who I knew quite well and for much longer than Ken.

I was annoyed at this turn of events and quite frankly angered.

When he visited other locations, Ken told those he met that Al and I were mismanaging the office. The implication in the conversations that made their way back to us was that had Ken been in charge, this of course would not be the case.

Ken also had a wide network of contacts in the business, and unbeknownst to us he was writing emails and letters that attacked our reputations. When his colleagues and friends visited and I was the host, Ken told them "in confidence" that I was unqualified for my job. It was difficult to pretend that I did not know what he was doing, but I refused to let Ken's unprofessional conduct create enmity between myself and our visitors. I remained upbeat and professional, trusting that Ken's colleagues would question his judgment and in turn his motives. I suggested to Al that Ken could not be trusted and should not be permitted to go on travel in a role where he represented the office. It had already reached the point where both Dick and I refused to travel with Ken on tour. Al took this advice and only let Ken play an official role if he was present and Ken was under his supervision. Of course Al could not watch Ken constantly, so it was unclear whether this really had any impact. But it did prevent Ken from taking the more active outreach role intended for his position.

Ken would approach a group after an office activity and use the discussions to say something negative about me. It might concern a presentation that I gave or something that I said or a program that I organized. He would phrase the comment in a way that required a response from the people he was speaking to, and he usually managed to elicit a reply. Any reply was sufficient for his purposes, and he used the opportunity to approach me personally to say that he had spoken to people in the audience and that they did not like my presentation or did not like something that I said. The implication, of course, was that they had sought him out to make their point. He would also use Al's meetings to announce that he heard negative comments about programs that I organized. I was forced repeatedly to defend myself, recounting the anecdotal evidence I had received that indicated precisely the opposite. Fortunately, others at the meetings typically recited supporting evidence in my favor. I also had a colleague who regularly attended my presentations for the purpose of providing me with personal feedback, and his comments would run counter to

Ken's. We used surveys and analyses for each event, and they too refuted Ken's claims. But none of that really seemed to matter. Ken had achieved his purpose of denigrating me either personally or in front of the group.

I completed several research projects, which were widely vetted by the broader business community of which we were a part. He would challenge their value at meetings, but when pressed had no constructive criticism and refused to put his comments in writing.

"You wouldn't take my criticism seriously, anyway," he said.

I found myself overreacting to almost everything Ken said, and my wife brought it to my attention after I embarrassed myself by overreacting to a comment from Ken in front of a prominent guest at a social event. I realized she was right, and I was angry at myself that Ken's malicious conduct was succeeding in bringing out the worst in me.

That occasion was a turning point, and Ken's misbehavior lost its impact. This change was important to my psyche and allowed me to step back and respond unemotionally to Ken's constant antagonism.

Ken's opposition became an expected part of any proposal I made, much like one of Pavlov's dogs. Eyes rolled and knowing looks were exchanged when Ken took the floor to give a view that was typically the complete opposite of what I proposed.

Ken visited another office at Al's direction to consult

with them on an upcoming project, and Ken made sure that everyone knew that the only reason he was there was because of Al's wish for people to believe that our office was "taking action" on an issue that Al thought was important, when according to Ken there really was not a need for it. Ben had been with Ken on the trip, and he came to me completely exasperated.

"I do not want to travel with Ken ever again. He is embarrassing. The director of the office we visited came to me privately because his people were worried that Ken was unhappy and that they weren't meeting our expectations."

"What was the issue?" I asked.

"Every meeting we went to Ken told the group that the only reason we were there was because Al was into actionism."

"Actionism? What is that supposed to mean?"

 "I don't know. He never explained it. I was so upset that I wrote the trip report myself so you'd know that our visit was productive."

Ken made it a point to intimidate others who he perceived were supportive of Al and me. He could become angry in an instant.

His anger did not work with me, so with me he was indirect: he glared. I would look his way during a meeting, a working lunch, or an activity only to find him glaring at me. The first time I noticed he was staring, I thought that I had "caught" him looking at me. But it happened virtually every time we were at an event together, and he made it a point to make sure that I noticed. Whenever I spoke in front of a group and he was present, he put himself in my line of sight so that I would have to make eye contact, and he always glared.

I suppose he believed that his angry stare would have an unsettling effect. Instead, it was just one more indication to me that Ken was, to use clinical slang that the psychology profession does not like, simply crazy. I concluded that he could not help himself. While this made me feel better, the realization did nothing to stop the behavior.

This strange conduct helped me not to be surprised by nearly anything that he did, but even I was not prepared for what I found after I washed my car one warm summer day.

I had been taking my car to the car wash when it was dirty, but on a particularly nice day I decided to wash it myself. My car was new, and for the most part I parked it either at home in the garage or at work. As I dried the car off with a towel, I noticed that the right side of my car was completely covered with deep nicks and small dents. We had reserved spaces at work, and Ken parked in the slot directly to my right. He had an old four door and carried his work in the back seat, so he had an "excuse" to open both doors on the driver's side of his car. I began to park on the very left of my slot. I had Al's car off to my left, and I wondered if he might ask why I was crowding his space. He never did.

Because Al did his best to remain neutral when Ken and I clashed, Ken's unprofessional conduct not only continued but escalated.

It would eventually breach the threshold of unethical behavior.

Ken would not let his people support initiatives of which he did not personally approve. I tried to get Al to reallocate people into a central planning cell so that Ken could not hamper our effectiveness, but Al was not up for the fight to take people away from Dick, Ned and Ken to build the new group. We never did get planning right, and Ken was usually able to derail any event he decided he did not like.

On one occasion, Al insisted on hosting a particular event despite Ken's suggestion that there was insufficient time to prepare for it. Ken refused to give it any of his support and when it looked like the event would be a disaster, Ken gloated and expressed privately to a colleague that he hoped the office — and specifically Al — would be embarrassed. Fortunately, one of the staff members made the necessary effort to get the event back on track, and it was subsequently acknowledged as a resounding success.

Bypassing His Boss

Al came up with the idea to bring recently retired senior leaders within the company to our office to speak to the participants on the six-month course. The purpose was to let them talk about lessons learned while they were with the company, things they would do differently if given the chance, what challenges they believed were still to be solved, and finally to talk about the most important issue of their tenure.

He assigned Ken's division the job to organize the

event. Ken took the task on enthusiastically because it gave him an opportunity to talk to some of the most important people in the business. As he had a full-time assistant to help him do the grunt work, Ken was able to devote himself to making phone calls and to revel in the rubbing of elbows with high-level people "just like him".

Ken and Al traded emails throughout the preparation for the event, and I merely monitored the exchanges unless I had something I wanted to interject.

When the event finally took place, it was a tremendous success. Both the participants on the six-month course and the retirees thought it had been a brilliant occasion. It was so brilliant, in fact, that Ken could not resist declaring the entire affair had been his idea.

Al wanted to repeat the event, and Ken enthusiastically volunteered to take it on again. He had devised a way to get himself on stage with the senior executives and play a central role as moderator.

But the events had a side effect: Ken began corresponding directly with Al on all issues, including those that were under my purview. I reacted strongly, but as per usual Ken ignored my objections. I went to Al and asked that he "push" issues back down to me when Ken sent them up without any opportunity for me to comment. Al did this for awhile, but then he tired of it and took the easy way out: He just answered Ken's emails directly, often making decisions that were not his to make.

I went to Al again, and once more he pushed issues down to my level when Ken tried to bypass me. But Al yet again tired of the "game" and took the path of least resistance to avoid conflict with Ken.

This is another hallmark of narcissists. They have incredible fortitude and tenacity when it comes to conflict and getting their way. I often went home feeling like giving up. I would have to regroup in the evening to regain my equilibrium and determination to carry on the next day, knowing that disagreement with Ken was inevitable.

I ended up being more or less sidelined when it came to exercising decisions that involved Ken. *De facto* Ken was working for Al.

Without Al's support, I felt that I had to let things go as long as I agreed with the way issues played out, intervening only when I did not like the direction they were taking. It was a compromise that I tacitly agreed to, but not one that I was happy about.

Ken also began to insert himself in places where he had no role or responsibility.

He set up a meeting to develop objectives for a high visibility conference that was my responsibility. When Al was briefed by Ken, he made the assumption that I had delegated the task, and of course Ken was not about to make him think otherwise. When I realized what had happened, I had to assert myself when it should not have been necessary.

Ken unashamedly took advantage of new arrivals who did not know the normal routine.

We sponsored a conference twice a year that by tradition the Director opened with welcoming remarks. We had diligently worked to increase attendance, so I had a special affinity for the people who attended. Ken's group organized it, and Gil, who was new to the office, was the primary coordinator. When I showed up to make my remarks, Gil informed me that Ken was making them.

"Ken is making the remarks? Who made that decision?" I asked, feeling strangely annoyed and surprised at the same time.

Gil crossed his arms. "I decided to spread the wealth when it comes to who makes the opening remarks at our conferences."

"Don't you think it would have been appropriate to inform me of your intentions?" I asked.
Ken was watching us talk, and he did not hide his smirk.

The welcoming remarks were supposed to be brief and directed at the participants, emphasizing the importance of their participation to our organization and our appreciation for their presence. Ken instead talked about himself for ten minutes, outlining his professional career and the very long list of responsibilities that he held at our office. He never did acknowledge the participants. It was a surreal performance.

I let Gil know that next time, and every time, I — or whoever was the Director — would be making the opening remarks.

Ken continued to disrupt the office and make the

people around him miserable. If he served on a selection board for new hires, invariably he would not support the candidate the rest of the board agreed was best. Consequently, every board of which he was a part was delayed while he wrote letters to Al, demanding that his advice be followed and that the recommendation of the rest of the selection team be overridden. Al's solution was to stop assigning Ken to serve on selection boards — which, while avoiding confrontation, only served to fuel Ken's anger.

Ken often went to Al's office to complain about how his talents were not properly appreciated, and the two of them would end up in screaming matches. For me, this kind of interaction between a subordinate and a corporate VP was unprecedented, and I could not understand why Al tolerated Ken's disrespectful misconduct.

A member of the Board had come up with a project that he thought our office should implement on behalf of the company. We had a layered Board structure, and the Board member took his idea to the Senior Board to get their buy-in. It was an ambitious venture, and Al was pleased to have our office selected as the one to "make it happen". He had heard that this might be coming, and he had obviously given much consideration to who should be in charge of the task.

"I've decided to give this project to Ken," Al confided to Dick and me at our Tuesday morning meeting. "It'll keep him busy and give him the chance to use his experience and knowledge. He did a good job on the retiree seminar, and I think he'll do well on this, too."

Ken loved organizing the retiree seminar because it meant he got to hang around with important people. That element was missing on this project. Ken also had Bob to do all the grunt work while he limited his involvement to the high-visibility aspects of the event. Bob was not part of this effort, and this task would require extensive project management, curriculum development, follow-up and oversight. Ken had not shown that any one of these traits was a *forte* of his.

In the end, Al miscalculated. What neither of us foresaw was that his miscalculation would lead to total war.

From Conduit to Bottleneck

Ken's office was responsible for the flow of information from the action teams up to first me, and then Al. The routine was straightforward: we had an event, Ken's team developed the after action review which included feedback from the participants, and it was sent up so that Al and I could see the in-house assessment of how the current program was perceived, the intentions for the future, and recommendations for change. It was on the change aspects that Al and I concentrated. Should there be systemic change, should the objectives be updated, and what should stay the same? Our goal was to keep our program current and more importantly relevant to the interests of the audience. Al and I kept apprised of the preparation, observed the program's execution, and our comments in the context of the assessment by Ken's team were the way that we influenced the program's content and conduct.

Lenny kept the momentum going for the first nine months or so after Ken's arrival, but once Lenny left and Ken was in the office and "in charge", compliance with the schedule deteriorated.

What also happened was that Ken began implementing change that in Al's and my view reflected not the best interests of the program, but instead served Ken's personal agenda. Hence our comments to the assessments began to reflect not just our observations on the program, but our criticism of his judgment.

As the combined impact of inefficiency and criticism gained traction, the information flow from Ken's level to ours began to wane. The weekly flow turned first to weeks and then a month and then nearly two months.

Ken's office went from conduit to bottleneck.

While I had heard about it, I did not really understand what projection was until I worked with Ken. The dictionary defines it this way: *the attribution of one's own ideas, feelings, or attitudes to other people; the externalization of blame, guilt, or responsibility as a defense against anxiety.*[5]

Ken began accusing me of the very activities in which he was involved. At first this struck me as strange, then bizarre, and eventually as outlandish as he began to lash out at any criticism directed his way.

---

[5] Merriam-Webster's Collegiate Dictionary, Eleventh Edition (2003), p 993.

Ken was responsible for the speakers who attended our major conferences. If I suggested that we consider a particular speaker, he accused me of inviting friends to come speak to the audience. But the truth was that he was eliminating existing speakers from our established six-month program and inviting old friends and former colleagues. Greeting a former colleague he invited to lecture he said, "Welcome — just as I promised."

When the participants on the six-month course "panned" his friends in the post-event survey, which happened often, he changed the assessment process so that the audience's opinion was ignored when his associates were criticized. With the incessant delays making it impossible for Al and me to provide timely input and Ken's "new system" in place, the assessment process became so arbitrary that only Ken's opinion counted.

We had a highly successful annual conference attended by many of the graduates of our six-month course, and Ken demanded that we "formalize" its organization so that he could set proper milestones. I stressed that we already had a well defined process and that all he needed to do was follow it.

As the program fell under Ken, the organizers had to go to him for input. Ken stubbornly refused to provide the needed information. Repeatedly Al and I and others raised the issue at Al's meetings, and Ken said he was working the issue. I talked to Ken's people offline and received assurances from them that the necessary information would be forthcoming.

It never did.

It turned out that Ken's people had been sending him information for months, and Ken had sat on it. Five months later and with the organizers desperate for the agenda, I finally intervened and put together the information that was needed to move the .program forward. Ken, of course, pronounced that the system — and not he — was at fault for the delays.

Ken's inaction reflected a pattern of information withholding and obstructionism that he practiced religiously.

Ken demanded that any information produced by his team, including that in support of Al and me, be sent up through him for his personal review. After already proving that he could not keep up with the production of his division, this was a recipe for disaster. Unable to work directly with electronic copies of documents, Ken ordered his secretary to create huge paper files for him to carry around. Paper copies of documents from other offices that were circulated through Ken started disappearing. Ben likened sending anything to Ken for his review as dumping it into a "black hole".

I sent reminders to Ken asking for products when they were due. Ken would in turn remind me that his division's workload was extremely heavy, that he lacked the people and resources to meet expectations, and that the tardiness was not his fault.

Ken withheld minutes of meetings conducted by the staff in his division that he knew I wanted expedited. By the time I received them, the subsequent cycle of events was already in motion. This was especially true of the research division, where we had some significant issues that we were trying to resolve.

When I put pressure on him to deliver the material on time, Ken began aggregating the documents and delivering them all at once to my office late on Friday, with the word "urgent" clearly marked on the front. If he could, he delivered the stacks of material the Friday before the Monday I was scheduled to be on travel.

Ken began sending long emotional diatribes on email to Al and me late in the evening as he left for the weekend or traveled out of town. It wasn't unusual on Mondays to have our mailboxes filled with bile. At first I felt compelled to respond to them because they were so outrageous, but when I realized that this was what Ken was hoping for — he knew a careful reply would require time to write — I began ignoring them. I pushed his emails off to the side, scanning them only after I covered all other traffic. Their content completely unpredictable, I mentally began writing off anything that Ken sent forward unless it was important to the function of the organization.

Al became so frustrated with Ken's inefficiency that he called him into his office to let him know how displeased he was. The screaming matches resumed, and Al began suffering from migraine headaches. He started missing work.

Al's wife came to mine and complained bitterly about "that man". She had been in the outer office during one of Al and Ken's screaming matches.

"I have never heard my husband raise his voice even

once in our marriage," she said. "This situation is unbelievable." She worried about Al and began demanding that he change his routine and diet, that he exercise more, and that they start getting away on the weekends.

Ken, meanwhile, seemed unaffected, even relishing the opportunity to debate Al on every issue and nuance of which he could possibly think. He began scheduling meetings with Al whose only apparent purpose was to argue.

It was not a surprise when Al told me that Ken blamed the existing set of circumstances, his strained relationship with Al included, on me. I sensed that Al believed it to some degree.

The whole situation turned out to be one of those times where you thought things could not get any worse, but the truth was that the downward plunge had just begun.

CHAPTER FOUR

Total War

Conflict was almost continuous. My departure was on the horizon, and I had hoped that Ken would back off knowing that it was only a matter of time until I was gone. But he seemed intent on making sure that I and everyone else knew that his actions these last eighteen months had been justified. He even seemed to have Al convinced that once I left, the atmosphere in the office would improve. Al's wife, on the other hand, worried what would happen with my departure.

For the sake of the office, I actually hoped that Ken was right. In particular, I hoped that he would behave differently once I was no longer in place.

The power of a narcissist is that he undermines your confidence. I blamed myself for what I was sure had to be my part in creating the dysfunctional relationship between Ken and me. I questioned my leadership, my management ability — this despite over 30 years of having achieved success and notoriety in every endeavor in which I was ever involved. I went over in my mind repeatedly what I might have done differently as an antidote to our poisoned interaction.

For his part, Ken never wondered what happened. He was absolutely sure the state of affairs had nothing to do with him — and said so to anyone who listened.

But it was Al's previous decision to give Ken responsibility for the new project sponsored by the Board that would ignite the flames of total war.

Ken sent emails to people across the company with great flourish shortly after Al gave him the "lead" for the new project. But that was the extent of it. Without anyone to push ahead on his behalf, and with the rest of the company looking to Ken to provide leadership, complete inertia was inevitable.

Every weekly meeting Al asked Ken for a status report and an overview of the way ahead, and Ken would allude to the emails that he had sent and the meetings he intended to hold when finally everyone would be available — meetings which were never scheduled — as evidence that the project was underway.

The project came out in November, Al assigned it to Ken a few weeks later, and the weeks turned into months with Ken taking no initiative to begin even preliminary discussions.

Al, who was ultimately accountable to the Board, was becoming anxious, and he tried repeatedly to get Ken to develop the sense of urgency needed if the project was to succeed. It was no surprise that the harder Al pushed, the more Ken resisted. Al finally directed Ken and Ben to visit another organization that served a clientele similar to that which our project would address, but Ken was more interested in making sure that everyone at the other organization knew that Al was more into "actionism", as he called it, than substance.

Al even became the victim of his own sense of urgency.

"The next item on the agenda is the new project," Al said at his weekly meeting. "What's the status?" He looked expectantly at Ken.

"Did you read my report?" Ken asked. He was referring to the report that Ben wrote.

"Of course I read the report," Al replied. "But what's the next step? How does the project become a reality? What is being planned? What is the schedule? What has actually been done?"

Ken's response was to sulk, insulted by questions that in his mind were unjustified personal attacks.

Dick collected documents the Board was sending us as a means of keeping us appraised of its discussions and expectations. When Dick showed them to me, I asked if Ken had seen them.

"I told him I put them into a folder, but he never came to get it." I took a look at the documents in the folder that Dick had organized. The Board was thinking big. We, on the other hand, weren't thinking at all.

I resisted the urge to intervene. When Al complained to Dick and me privately, I only nodded. This was Al's decision, the project was Ken's baby, and I was not going to get in the middle of it.

I have to admit that I was gloating a little. OK, I confess I was gloating a lot. Watching Ken do nothing, when there was so much to do, was giving me sheer pleasure.

Dick came into my office. As head of HR, he processed all the leave and travel requests for the senior staff. "Take a look at this and tell me what you think."

It was Ken's projected business travel and his leave request for the next seven months. He was asking for 43 workdays. Including weekends and holidays, the number of days he would be absent from the area was well over 80. It wasn't uncommon for Ken to take two weeks of sick leave every six months or so for medical appointments. A quick calculation told me that Ken could easily be gone for three of the next seven months.

I thought of the project that Ken was supposed to be leading. It had the attention of the Senior Board members. It had been proclaimed by the company in communiqués and press releases. Pulling together a plan would be a fulltime job for the next six months for whoever led it, especially since up to now utterly nothing had been accomplished.

Al was livid when Dick passed him Ken's request.

My concern for the organization and my earlier resolve not to let Ken embarrass the office again got the better of my judgment. After all, I had helped the Board develop the initial idea for the project, so I had strong opinions about its direction and objectives — and a desire to see it succeed. When Al finally expressed his deep frustration to Dick and me, angry and feeling helpless, I suggested that he reassign the project to me.

"Time is running out," I said. "Nothing has happened. If you leave this with Ken, nothing will. And all of us will suffer."

Little did I know that suffering was unavoidable and that we were just discussing the source.

Al was relieved that I volunteered. Dick happily handed me his file of documents.

"I'll tell Ken that I'm forming a committee to take on the project," Al said, "and that you're going to lead the team."

I nodded. "I'd like you to be clear with Ken that this was your decision — that you decided to make me the lead because of his inaction. He's got to know why you've taken the project away from him." Al agreed to this condition. But he would not keep his promise.

The weekend passed, and Al came to me early the next week. "I told Ken that I was going to create a new team to take on the project. I told him that I understood how busy he is and why he hasn't been able to devote the time needed to get the project off the ground, given the upcoming retiree seminar and all the other obligations he and his team have. He seemed OK with that explanation."

"Why wouldn't he?" I thought.

"Did you at least tell him that you decided to appoint me as the team lead?" I asked.

Al shook his head. "I didn't think it was necessary." But of course it was.

When Ker discovered that I was now leading the project, the earth shook. Or if it did not, it should have as a warning of what was to come.

Desolation

I have to confess some relief at finally having a project that would occupy my time and limit my interaction with Ken. Al was also enjoying the increased contact with the lower levels of the management structure, and as long as I was being copied on email traffic and I was informed of their activities, I let it go.

Ben confided to my wife that I appeared to be happy now that I had a project, and he was right.

There was substantial overlap between the goals of the project and the work of Ken's people. The foundation for conflict was present, which in our case made it unavoidable.

I was leaving my position at the end of the year and had no dog in the hunt as one of my colleagues used to say, so I developed a proposal that I believed would best serve the organization. Ken, of course, thought that the project should be used to enlarge his area.

But it was a new focus that we had not explored before in detail; required new skills and expertise; and required people more like those in the research division than the staff members who worked for Ken. We also received direction from the Board that made integrating the new people under Ken less than optimal, and the only physical location available in the building for the new program was on the same floor as the research division. All these reasons led Al and me to conclude that the new group was more suitably co-located with the research division than under Ken.

I laid out a plan where Ken's people would have a role in the early stages of the project, because we intended to reuse material his people were already tasked with creating. But aside from this, later development in my view had to be accomplished by others who were experts in the field.

I suggested that we should use outside expertise to develop the program's content incrementally until we got our own people in place, and I mapped out a detailed 2-year project management plan that built out the program from a short two weeks to ten. Given the time required to get all the approvals, Al and I agreed that trying to get the funding and people and build the infrastructure any more quickly was impractical.

Ken was incensed that he was not consulted on the "way ahead" since he had been designated originally as the lead. I tired of his using every opportunity to either criticize the work and decisions of the planning team or to complain that his division was being ignored. I finally told him that he had had months to take the program in any direction that he wanted, but that his neglect finally caused Al to take the project away from him. Ken was quick to recite what Al said and that I was misinformed.

Total war had begun.

The criticism of Al and me by Ken became

ubiquitous. He made outbursts in the lunch line, comments to visitors at hosted tables, and in several cases according to witnesses just just "lost it".

Al began confronting Ken and demanded that he stop his public comments. Ken ignored him.

Al, Dick and I met weekly on Tuesdays to establish a single view on the major issues in the office. It was often a strategy session on how to "handle" Ken.

Ken's conduct eventually became so offensive that reports of his inappropriate comments were reaching me almost daily. I began sending an email to Ken coincident with each incident, directing him to stop his criticism. But instead of stopping his criticism, Ken's response was to accuse me of defamation.

In the midst of all the nasty exchanges, Ken sent me a cordial email wishing me Happy Birthday. When I showed it to my wife, she said, "What did you expect?"

"What do you mean what did I expect? Is he nuts?"

"Psychologists don't use the term 'nuts'."

"So he's crazy."

"No, he's mentally ill."

"So you are saying he's nuts."

Al sent me a description of a narcissist that he downloaded from the Internet and suggested that it described Ken. I wondered if he had forgotten our earlier conversation. But I was happy that he at least finally seemed to recognize that Ken had an actual personality disorder.

It would be an email that he sent to both Al and me threatening legal action against us for defamation that I thought would finally seal Ken's fate. Al still refused to take action, and only after a subsequent email to me alluding to physical harm if I did not apologize for defaming his reputation, was Al finally compelled to act.

Al contacted a member of the Board who he knew quite well and said that he wanted Ken removed. He contacted the Head of the Board to tell him of his decision. In the end, Al was asked to give Ken one more chance.

When Al informed me that he had agreed to let Ken stay, I literally felt my head spin.

Al called Ken into his office and told him that "it was finished" and that any further emails or comments would result in his immediate removal. Al came to me and said if Ken so much as sent a single obnoxious email that he wanted to know.

Ken was more discrete in his criticism, but it still went on. He began to use his people as sounding boards since he could no longer spew his bile on others who might report it.

When I left my position, Ken was still in place. Ken felt exonerated at my departure and sent me an email that said, "The nightmare is finally over." How right he was.

CHAPTER FIVE

Looking Back

I did not think about my job for many months after I left. That's never been a tendency of mine anyway, as I am always looking to the future and the next opportunity.

My wife and I were also moving back into our old house that we had left vacant for three years while I worked the job with Al. I took 30 days off and worked on the house and yard, shopped for some new furniture with my wife, and reconnected with the kids who had not followed us to what was then our new location.

I decided to write this book six months after returning home. I had lost the disappointment that I felt for Al having taken no action, and I was no longer resentful that Ken was allowed to spoil what should have been the best job of my career.

More than anything, I needed as part of the writing process to ponder whether I could have done something that might have made a difference with Ken. The bottom line from my perspective is this:

After much reflection, it is my conviction that narcissists should be removed from the workplace when they reveal themselves. There is nothing they can offer that exceeds the damage they will do not only to your organization but to those who must work with them.

But I am also aware that there are narcissists who reach the top and can't be removed. And we are stuck working for them. They may be charismatic and brilliant — and to outsiders who do not have to associate closely with them they may indeed appear to be impressive people.

There have been many examples of people in the news who have exhibited significant narcissistic tendencies, including high profile political figures, Hollywood stars and prominent religious leaders.

Characteristics they displayed that are common to narcissists were numerous: the disconnect between their private lives and their public personas, which implies a lack of self-examination; the fact that they abused the trust that others placed in them in pursuit of unethical, immoral and even illegal self-serving behavior; the fact that they excoriated others for practicing the very same behavior they themselves indulged in; their tragic disregard for the emotional wellbeing of their spouses and families should their behavior eventually — perhaps inevitably is a better word given the many audit trails that exist today — come to light; and finally, a failure to acknowledge their wrongdoing when confronted with irrefutable evidence.

When the private lives of these individuals collide with their public façades, the result for them and everyone around them is catastrophe.

But many narcissists do not self-destruct. And of course, not all of us can leave our jobs just because a narcissist happens to arrive in the office. For those of you who find yourselves "stuck" in the company of a narcissist, the rest of this chapter is for you.

What to Expect from a Narcissist

The narcissist is a destructive personality.

He is arrogant. He is incapable of "hearing" others.

He is unprofessional and indulges in unethical practices. He does not respond when others appeal to reason or to common decency.

When the narcissist cannot intimidate, he is critical. When his criticism is confronted, he is insubordinate. When insubordination does not work, he threatens "legal" action.

A narcissist cannot be trusted to represent his organization because he cannot resist the temptation to criticize his superiors. He believes that he should be occupying the most important positions in his company and has the distorted perception that criticizing his superiors aggrandizes him. His lack of regard for others prevents him from understanding that open and self-serving criticism is disloyal and a violation of faith.

Despite repeatedly confronting him directly about his conduct, Al's conversations with Ken did not make a difference for longer than a few weeks. Any normal senior executive, confronted by the Vice President he works for, would respond with respect and humility, and change his behavior. Ken did not. More importantly, he could not.

When an individual reaches a certain level in his career, he no longer receives the immediate "rewards" that he did while still working his way up in the organization. The "pats on the back" and the quarterly recognition go away.

At the executive level, we might never be told that we are doing our jobs well. Instead, personal rewards come in the form of the people who work for us receiving special recognition because our organization performed capably. They come in the form of our being granted ever more opportunities and responsibilities, higher status and higher pay.

The narcissist, however, never outgrows the need for pats on the back and being explicitly told that he personally is doing a good job. That is why when an event is recognized as being extraordinary, he can't resist taking the credit and basking in the accolades.

When Al first decided to explore what it would mean to have Ken removed, he was advised that it would be difficult. This advice, although not the only factor, led Al to take no formal action. The good that could have been accomplished by Al removing Ken would have dwarfed any difficulties or objections from the Board.

I thought in the end as the time drew near for my departure that Ken would let me go quietly into the night. But that is not the narcissist's style. He plays no-holds-barred until the very end, and an intelligent and articulate narcissist may be the shrewdest and most devious personality one will ever encounter. The *modus operandi* of the narcissist is to continuously antagonize those he does not like.

If you never work with a narcissist, count your blessings.

I believe that narcissism will be common in this next

generation of young people. They are not challenged by their teachers, they take their quality of life for granted, and they are rewarded not for performance, but "just for showing up". The Internet, where forums like *You Tube* and *Facebook.com* allow everyone to post information about themselves so that anyone in the world has the chance to view it — regardless of its veracity — fosters narcissism. *You Tube* describes its venue as a place to "Broadcast Yourself", and an entertaining video may be viewed a half million times or more on *You Tube* in a single week. *Facebook.com* describes itself as "a place for friends", where people place innumerable pictures of their families and themselves and blog endlessly to their imaginary audiences.

So while you may not work with a narcissist now, I predict that the opportunity will become more common as today's young people grow up and move into the workplace.

Ten Rules for How to Deal with a Narcissist

It's not a perfect world, and perhaps leaving your job because a narcissist happens to show up in your office just isn't possible.

Maybe your job benefits are too good. Maybe you can't afford a pay cut. Maybe you'd have to move and you'd never be able to sell your house, or you love the school your kids attend. Maybe the economy isn't doing that great. Maybe you refuse to let that guy or gal run you out of the office. Maybe you just love your job despite the narcissist. Or perhaps there are a dozen other "maybes" that make it impossible for you to take another job.

So what do you do if the management in your office decides not to remove your narcissistic coworker, and you simply can't afford to leave your job?

Initially I was not aware of the extent of what I could only characterize as Ken's mental problems. I mistakenly thought that one could reason with him. Let me be crystal clear.

Reasoning with a narcissist is impossible. This realization is crucial, for it forms the basis for how best to deal with a narcissistic personality.

Let's discuss the implications of this observation by establishing "Ten Rules for How to Deal with a Narcissist". You will recognize Rule Number One.

Rule Number One: *do not attempt to reason with a narcissist.*

Both Al and I made the mistake of trying to reason with Ken. We thought when we discussed issues that he was listening, that he was open to other ideas or could be persuaded to take a different view of an issue when evidence suggested that his perspective deserved reexamination.

A narcissist is not open to other people's ideas.

We must realize that the narcissist views every situation as a "zero sum game". If you receive praise, then there is less for him. If he concedes an argument, then that means you "won" and he "lost". If he accepts criticism, it shames him. If he allows himself to be held accountable, he must admit that he was wrong.

The point is that every situation, regardless of its context, must make the narcissist feel better about himself if he is to accept the outcome. This, of course, is unlikely — let's be honest and admit that it is impossible — and therefore conflict is inevitable.

A normal person cannot understand the rage a narcissist feels, because normal people do not perceive every comment — particularly well-intended criticism — as a potential personal attack. The narcissist, on the other hand, overreacts to even the mildest criticism. He will spend hours writing long letters and rambing emails to rationalize his actions or misconduct. He will attack others harshly without warning or justification.

Al and I repeatedly tried to confront Ken's misconduct. But when you think about it, being confronted about misconduct for the narcissist is a combination of losing an argument, being criticized, and accepting accountability. It turns out that confronting a narcissist is fraught with potholes, and if not handled properly can lead to verbal combat and repercussions for the one who tries, even gently, to raise an issue that questions the competence or motives of the narcissist.

This leads me to Rule Number Two.

Rule Number Two: *never confront a narcissist about his misconduct when the two of you are alone.*

I was taught that good managers do not criticize their subordinates publicly. It harms the morale of not only the person involved, but also the morale of the organization because of the impression that public correction may make on others. Taking your subordinate aside and quietly confronting him alone was deemed the right approach.

Let me be candid. This well-considered approach to managing people does not apply to a narcissist. Narcissists always criticize others openly and in public, and the same technique must be used on them to have effect.

After my first "counseling session" with Ken, I should have dropped any attempts to meet with him alone. Foolishly, I continued to apply management strategies that were inadequate for the circumstances.

Confrontation when tried alone may also lead to a situation where the narcissist misinterprets what was said. With his penchant for spreading his displeasure when it suits his agenda, his perception of the conversation will become common knowledge very quickly. If you take issue with his explanation after having had a private conversation, it becomes your word against his.

Neither are you likely to gain any ground by confronting the narcissist with even the most persuasive argument or the most compelling evidence when you have a one-on-one dialogue. This is because the narcissist does not dialogue, he monologues.

For the narcissist, facts are debatable. Anecdotal evidence that the narcissist "wants" to believe is more compelling than any objective analysis.

When confronted with his misconduct, the narcissist

will try to change the subject and make the debate about something that he believes will put his adversary on the defensive. He will ignore the point you are trying to make, or perhaps more accurately will fail to see why your point even matters.

To break through the barrier that a narcissist erects around himself, confrontation should always be done in groups of at least three (the narcissist plus two), and larger settings such as meetings are even better. There is safety in numbers, and by confronting the narcissist in a group, others who identify with your frustration will be able to find their voices and back your assertions. You will also be insulated from counterattacks, and the "leader" of the meeting can referee and keep comments from getting out of hand.

For example, a participant at a meeting might refer to a particular behavior of the narcissist, while not referring to him directly. I should have in one of Al's meetings raised etiquette in the auditorium and how I believed it was rude for people in the audience to talk while someone was giving a presentation. That would have allowed others to agree and reinforce my initial comments while offering their own perspective on the issue, and for Al to "decree" that talking in the auditorium should be the exception. Hence Ken's behavior could have been confronted as unacceptable, and the pain of trying to convey this privately avoided.

If at all possible, managers should also avoid confronting narcissists alone. It is more effective to pick a battle and raise the issue in a meeting. Even if it makes the group uncomfortable because the comments may be personal, only the "weight" of the group can engender change.

Al used his meetings effectively in this regard. He never attacked Ken directly, but rather focused on the tasks for which Ken was responsible. He treated the situation as if each task had a life of its own independent of Ken, which allowed him to press Ken hard for results. If Ken chose to make the issue personal, Al was then free to join in kind and suggest that Ken should reorganize either his schedule or his team as necessary to get the job done.

If the manager chooses a private setting for confronting the narcissist, he should be prepared for failure and for counterattacks. He must also be prepared to take unilateral corrective action when confrontation has no effect, which is the most likely outcome of a personal discussion aimed at changing behavior.

Al's private meetings with Ken inevitably led to verbal combat. He had more success when he brought the same issues to his weekly meetings for discussion in front of the group. The open setting required Ken to behave himself and address the matter at hand.

Sometimes the narcissist will approach others, even managers, when they are alone. He views it as an opportunity to antagonize those he does not like and to undermine the confidence of those he sees as competitors or threats to his self-esteem.

The narcissist may also decide that someone is useful in achieving his personal agenda. This person may not realize that he has been targeted and hence may be particularly vulnerable to the narcissist's manipulation.

Half truths and misleading statements are part of the narcissist's arsenal, and his personal comments directed at you — no matter how hurtful — should be kept in perspective.

This leads me to mention the very important Rule Number Three.

Rule Number Three: *set boundaries.*

No one has to be a victim.

For managers, this means setting deadlines to avoid becoming a victim of the narcissist's inaction. Having said that, setting deadlines alone may not be sufficient to get the narcissist to do something that he believes lesser beings should be doing. Ken tried to justify his inaction by claiming that he had neither the resources nor people to do his job. The manager will have to be prepared to announce in his meetings to the group that Task A is not being completed and to ask the narcissist directly what he is doing about it. The manager should keep a record of how many times he has asked the same question and announce this to the group as well. Whatever technique the manager decides to use, he should keep the narcissist in the spotlight until a satisfactory response is received.

If this sounds childish, that's because it is. Emotionally, a narcissist is like a rebellious teenager who needs constant oversight and supervision. This is the price the senior staff within an organization pays for not having the courage to remove the offender.

For his coworkers, setting boundaries refers to protecting their emotional wellbeing. *Disrespect and antagonism do not have to be tolerated.* Remember that it is not impolite to excuse oneself for an "appointment" or to use the restroom if the narcissist becomes aggressive or his conduct becomes uncomfortable.

When I discovered that Ken was antagonizing Hank, I failed to realize the degree of the antagonism. And when it reached the boiling point, it was too late. Hank was only a notch lower than Ken on the organizational chart, so he was well-seasoned. But like all of us, he had never faced a narcissist before. With utter disregard for Hank's professional aspirations, Ken destroyed Hank's motivation and ultimately weakened the organization.

Neither are you obligated to be the narcissist's friend. The danger of getting friendly with a narcissist is that he will be tempted to use you to accomplish his own agenda. You may find yourself getting dragged into conflict with others that you would never become involved in if given a choice.

Some of the staff under Ken found themselves getting between Ken and me, and I had to go to them personally to assure them that I understood they were not directly involved of their own accord.

The narcissist will do everything that he can to make professional arguments personal. The key, therefore, to keeping the narcissist at arm's length is to keep your relationship strictly professional and avoid personal exchanges. After learning that he had criticized me openly while on tour, I no longer socialized with Ken unless we were attending the same event organized by others. While I was always cordial, I avoided making personal comments of any kind and kept our interaction focused on professional issues.

Avoiding the narcissist sounds cold-blooded, but the truth is that he does not belong in a workplace where teamwork and harmony are important to its efficiency and effectiveness. Your first priority should be to protect yourself.

If you find later that you want to "reach out" to the narcissist, that of course is your prerogative. But when you find yourself listening to criticism of others that is unjustified or just downright ugly, you will have to address it. This of course, is Rule Number Four.

Rule Number Four: *let no negative action go unchallenged.*

The difficulty presented by Rule Number Four is that by the time you discover that the narcissist has conducted himself unprofessionally or unethically, a significant period of time may have already passed.

When my old boss called to tell me of Ken's misconduct on the tour, I should have asked him to call Al directly and put the onus on the guy at the top to address the problem. In retrospect, there was a conflict of interest, and I never should have dealt directly with Ken again until the situation was resolved above my pay grade. But I confess that the idea that Ken would do what my old boss accused him of struck both Al and me as bizarre, and because I had already planned to speak to him about other issues, Al was content to let me talk to Ken. I also have to admit that I believed once Ken realized that what he said was reported back to me, he would be embarrassed and never do it again.

I have to acknowledge now that I don't recall Ken being embarrassed or ashamed of his actions, only surprised that I found out he was being openly critical of me. In one of his very last emails before I left, Ken referred to the incident with my former boss and called it "gossip by a bystander in a party conversation." Having first the gall to refer to a former senior executive of the company as a mere bystander and gossiper, and second having never denied that what was reported to me was true, he still viewed the account of his inappropriate conduct as hearsay.

Sue, who came to me with the intent to file a complaint with HR, had the right idea. She had every intention of taking Ken to task for his actions. The fact that I convinced her to talk to Ken first to defuse the situation was something that I had done many times before in other workplaces to avoid escalating what might have been a mere misunderstanding, to a level where both parties may have regretted their actions.

But I had already witnessed Ken's misdeeds: his open criticism of me, his treatment of Hank and Dick, his unwillingness to listen to Lenny or me when it came to excessive travel and to Wally when it came to procedure. I failed to take into account the whole of Ken's interaction with others when Sue approached me, and instead focused only on this single incident. If I had it to do over, at a minimum I would go with Sue to Al as more evidence that Ken was not only ill-suited but should not be granted the privilege to work in our office. But the management strategies that we all learn as we make our way to the top are deeply ingrained.

This leads me to suggest Rule Number Five.

Rule Number Five: *normal management techniques do not work.*

When it comes to handling a narcissist, throw out the book on management techniques and break out the book on leadership.

The military academies are leadership laboratories that teach leadership skills. The military is very good at establishing "zero tolerance" for certain actions: sexual harassment, fraternization, drug use, disrespect for others, a lack of integrity, and what the Uniform Code of Military Justice calls conduct unbecoming an officer.

Many times there aren't legal grounds for taking action against an offender. But a military officer has both the responsibility and obligation to create an atmosphere where every individual under his authority has an opportunity to reach his potential and to perform his very best. Anything less hurts the team and in a combat setting can endanger lives. So when someone comes in and maliciously undermines the atmosphere, it is grounds for punitive action. This takes many forms and can even result in the reassignment of an individual if the offense warrants outright removal.

Zero tolerance should be the rule when dealing with a narcissist, and removal from the workplace should be management's first instinct. Delaying removal will only make it harder to justify terminating employment later. Extenuating circumstances must be convincing if there is to be a reprieve.

And if a reprieve is given, then I suggest that you follow Rule Number Six.

Rule Number Six: *keep a record.*

I should have kept a journal of every incident involving Ken. The problem, of course, is that I did not know in advance that I might need one. And when I finally did catalogue all the incidents to make the case to Al that Ken should be dismissed, I am sure that there were some compelling ones that I left out.

How many of us, you ask, have time to keep a journal that details the misconduct of someone else? Do I want someone keeping a journal about me that might be used to show that I should be fired?

Perhaps this rule is best directed at managers, but coworkers would be wise to keep a "bulletized" record of dates and incidents when they find themselves in conflict with a narcissist. Supporting emails should be retained and kept in a separate file.

Ken told me that he had compiled an entire notebook on me. Al was smart enough to have built a notebook detailing all that Ken had said to him. I, on the other hand, was the only one who wasn't prepared if the situation blew up into a formal investigation.

A record is what the legal counsel of your corporation will require, and an accurate record of events from your perspective will protect you from unfair repercussions.

One of the senior technical experts who worked for Ken came to me and said that he was "ordered" by Ken not to support me in any fashion. This, despite the need for us to collaborate on technical initiatives. Fortunately for me, he refused to be bullied and stated in no uncertain terms that he would reject what he considered unethical direction from a superior. This was one of the few times when Ken met his match, but he still went after the technician indirectly by giving the identical order to his supervisor. He, too, refused to follow Ken's direction.

If you make the conscious decision to defy the narcissist, then to keep your sanity you will need to remember Rule Number Seven.

Rule Number Seven: *expect criticism.*

There is no more savage critic than a narcissist who has decided that he does not like you.

You will be greatly disappointed when you hear about the criticism.

You will wonder why it is so incessant.

You will wonder at its ugliness.

You will want to cry, or to quit, or you will feel defeated.

It will frustrate you that your management will not stop it.

It will frustrate you that you cannot prevent it.

You will wonder what you did to cause it.

If you are not careful, you may lose sleep over it and even develop health problems.

Let me assure you that the criticism of you by the narcissist is not justified, and this leads me to write Rule Number Eight. Please read it carefully.

Rule Number Eight: *if the narcissist does not like you, do not worry — it is not about you.*

Narcissism is a personality disorder. Maladaptive behavior. Mental illness.

This is the good news, but it is hard to maintain your composure and "be yourself" when you know that someone is being allowed to criticize you and tarnish your reputation — regardless of whether he cannot help himself. I had let Ken's malicious behavior change my own for the worse, and it took my wife to bring me back to center. I offer this insight because I struggled with it deeply. I lost sleep over it. I wondered when things were at their worst with Ken if I triggered them or provoked Ken unnecessarily.

Normal people do not enjoy constant conflict with others. We all want and seek harmony, particularly in an office where we are obligated to work closely together. When there is one person who continuously sows discord, it is uncomfortable and even debilitating. It harms the efficiency of everyone and may even damage the collective reputation of the group.

When I tried to get along with Ken, he regarded my attempt to establish a constructive relationship as weakness and seemed to redouble his efforts to undermine me and my position. When I confronted his every action, he lashed out wildly in all directions. When I backed off from confronting him regularly, it made him bolder and more contentious.

There was no disposition, no approach, no posture that was workable.

I say this so if you find yourself helpless to find middle ground with the narcissist that you realize there is no middle ground. No compromise. This is the narcissist in full flower, and it's not about you. It's about him.

I was at a conference and met a colleague of Ken's. When I told him of our struggles, he told me that "Ken has done this with all his bosses." I guess I was more horrified that it had been allowed to go on for so long than I was surprised at this "revelation".

So let me say it again. It is not about you. And this leads me to Rule Number Nine.

Rule Number Nine: *it is OK to feel relief, even joy, when you and the narcissist finally part company.*

In hindsight, Al's predecessor was probably a narcissist, too.

I overlapped with Al's predecessor for about two months, and he was difficult. Back then I did not know what a narcissist was, but the giveaway in retrospect was that he spoke only in monologue. The only way to have a conversation, I learned, was to ask questions to guide the exchange so that he would eventually monologue about what you needed to know.

When we had staff meetings — he never willingly shared information and staff meetings were rare — he "monologued" the entire time, not asking for feedback or whether anyone had any issues they wanted to raise. He just was not interested. I found myself the only one asking questions, but as long as he was the only one giving answers, he did not seem to mind.

He treated people extremely poorly. He had very few supporters anywhere in the organization. My predecessor, who worked with him for three years, was miserable. His counterpart on the support side had been completely pushed aside, and the boss openly disdained him. If my predecessor had not liked the other people in the office so much, he told me it would have been a hopeless situation. He got to the point where he often took initiative without informing the boss, because the boss refused to delegate even the most elementary decisions.

A colleague from outside the office referred to Al's predecessor as "The King". It was truly *apropos*.

When it finally came time for Al's predecessor to leave, there was a tradition that all of us who had worked for him would line the hall from the elevator on the first floor to the exit leading to the street out in front of the building. It was a sort of gauntlet, and the boss walked through it, shaking hands with everyone and sharing a few personal words with each of us while bidding *adieu*. It was typically an emotional experience for the one leaving, and this was no exception. By the time Al's predecessor got through the gauntlet, he had tears in his eyes and could hardly speak. He walked out the door and into the waiting car. He waved bravely, choking back the emotion, as the car drove off.

When the car turned the corner and drove out of sight, shouting and clapping erupted. I watched in amazement as the entire group began cheering and singing and dancing. One of the longtime secretaries actually began dancing in a circle, and everyone laughed and clapped and stomped their feet. For a few moments, pandemonium reigned. The only thing missing was the sound of popping corks. The King was gone, and his departure was cause for celebration.

I must admit being appalled at the time, but I have to tell you that when I finally left the office after a full two years of dealing with Ken, I felt such great relief that I, too, celebrated the end of a difficult and personally harmful relationship.

I guess I am saying that sometimes our human nature gets the better of us. But we can't help ourselves when the oppression is finally lifted. *So I suggest that it's OK to feel relief, even joy, when the narcissist parts company.*

This leads to Rule Number Ten.

Rule Number Ten: *pick up the pieces and don't look back.*

I wondered when I took my next job if I could rejoin the workplace and enjoy it. I did not realize how much Ken affected me and how pervasive his negative influence had become until I left.

In my new job I kept waiting for the disharmony to come spilling out. I kept waiting for people to criticize and fight among themselves because of the friction created by one individual in a key position. But it has not happened. I am enjoying work again, finding myself having professional disagreements that do not become personal. Issues can be discussed and worked out, and there is reasonable discussion and compromise. Situations are no long zero sum games, and we are working toward a common goal. It is a pleasure.

So when the narcissist and you part company, be assured that you can enjoy work again. Your professional life is not over because of the narcissist. *Maybe in some ways, because of your experience, the real fun and enjoyment and appreciation for a healthy work environment has just begun.*

EPILOGUE

I want to make two points in closing.

The first is that if you are in conflict with a narcissist, you may discover that you are struggling alone. Others in the same office may have no appreciation of the battle in which you find yourself. This is primarily because the narcissist is clever — perhaps devious is a better word — in how he works. He attempts to isolate his adversary and speaks to others "in confidence" about his colleague's lack of competence and character. Al was skeptical when I first spoke to him about Ken because he was unaware of the constant confrontation. Longtime colleagues and friends of mine wondered why Ken and I could not get along. Around them Ken was sociable, pleasant and charming.

When Ken began sending me emails marked "personal and confidential", which were really nothing other than malicious diatribes, at first I answered them directly — and confidentially. But this opened the door for even greater malevolence, and I began first forwarding them to Al, then blindly copying Al on our interaction, and finally openly including Al in my responses so that Ken would know that he could not attack others "in secret" and with impunity.

My wife attended a conference of the American Counseling Association, and a highly successful woman was scheduled to speak to the group on a particular topic. But she was so distressed by the narcissistic personality she was working with that she could talk about nothing else. Instead of focusing on the planned subject, the speaker poured out her desperation to the audience of psychologists and counselors, and she appealed to the group for ideas on how to cope with the dysfunctional colleague in her office who was causing so much anguish. The sad truth was that even this educated audience did not "get it". My wife did, but only because she was intimately familiar with the struggles I had with Ken. But unless you have worked personally with a narcissist, it is difficult to understand or appreciate his impact on those around him.

We also need to recognize that the narcissist knows who he is, but those working with him for the first time do not. We believe that the narcissist is like our other coworkers, and it is a process of gradual discovery to finally realize who we are up against. By then much time may have passed and much conflict may have already roiled the office — and when we look back we may have handled the situation with less aplomb than we would have liked.

Bottom line? Do not expect empathy from your colleagues when you find yourself confronting a narcissist. Rather, begin using the rules I outlined to protect yourself — and if your management does nothing to help resolve the situation, you might want to consider looking for another job.

Second, I do not intend by sharing my story for people to start identifying every self-centered, demanding personality with narcissistic tendencies as having a personality disorder. Some people are born with a negative personality. We may not like them, but that does not make them narcissistic. In fact, the truly narcissistic personality is rare.

Let's face it. Some people are just plain ornery or self-serving or full of self-importance, but it does not mean that they have a personality disorder. They are just flawed people.

The same goes for know-it-alls, people who like to talk about themselves, and people who like to hear themselves talk. They may be unpleasant company, but they are not necessarily narcissists.

We typically try to label behaviors so that we better understand them, and this is particularly true of negative behaviors. What we should remember is that what separates the truly narcissistic personality from the difficult one is the malice associated with the narcissist's view of others.

It is malice that leads to constant conflict. It is malice that permits the narcissist to criticize and undermine his coworkers. It is malice that permits the narcissist to threaten bosses and attempt to tarnish their reputations. And it is malice that permits narcissists to further their own personal agendas at the expense of others and ultimately the organization which they are supposed to serve.

I offered ten rules for how to cope with a narcissist. Perhaps in closing I should add an eleventh.

Rule Number Eleven: *while many of us may have narcissistic tendencies, you can identify the true narcissist by how he regards others.*

If you're working with a narcissist, you have my deepest sympathies. But do not lose hope. Do not be discouraged. It is possible, using the rules I have suggested, to contain the damage the narcissist will try to inflict on you, your coworkers and your organization.

Enough said. Do not grow weary. Get out there and fight the good fight.

Dr. Samuel Grier has a long and distinguished record of public service with the U.S. Air Force, the North Atlantic Treaty Organization, the U.S. government and two Federally Funded Research and Development Centers.

He and his wife lived in Brussels, Belgium, for three years and Rome, Italy, for more than five. Sam's career has taken his family to a variety of locations they called home in the United States, and they have traveled Europe extensively. Sam has also traveled to Uganda and Northern Africa.

A prolific writer, Sam has authored and edited papers on foreign policy, terrorism, the future of conflict, education, computer science and missile defense.

Sam took an unexpected journey into the realm of the psychological, leading to his one work of non-fiction, Narcissism in the Workplace.

***

Fiction by Samuel Grier

Starr Chronicles:

Di Zhen
22 Lubianka Street

www.SamuelGrier.com

Made in the USA
Middletown, DE
26 October 2021